Prai

"*784* is a fun read loaded with character-building wisdom. Author James Ring switches gears from his previous book, *Necessary Assets*, an international thriller, and pens a poignant memoir of his early childhood visits to his family's greengrocer store and camp compound.

784 reveals how character is absorbed from caring family members. It is a well-deserved tribute to Ring's immigrant family and trio of first generation uncles including a small-town mayor and friend of President Franklin Delano Roosevelt. *784* seamlessly shares character lessons in a subtle manner that fosters honorable relationships and prudent risk taking."
– Kenneth R. O'Brien, The Profile Group

"This is a book to savor as one would enjoy a special occasion family meal. It demonstrates the power of love to form character for all generations. It is a terrific story. James Ring tells the story of his immigrant family through episodes from childhood memory, and through his reflections as a family man himself. He does so with humor, compassion, affection, and the skill of a wise teacher."

–The Reverend Susan Baker-Borjeson

"Jim Ring's new book about Kingston, New York, is a fascinating account of a time gone by, of an America quickly vanishing. Ring's sly way of telling the lessons he learned as a boy kept me riveted and reading. He made me feel his family was my family. It is such a wonderful story with rich details of unforgettable characters; it made me long for that America. It is a northern version of *Huckleberry Finn* and just as enchanting."
– Ron Gollobin, Retired Journalist

784 Broadway

A Remembrance

James Ring

Omni Publishing Co.

2015

Published by
Omni Publishing Co.
www.omni-pub.com

Library of Congress cataloging-in-publication data
Ring, James A.
784 Broadway
ISBN 978-1506164182
Printed in the United States of America
April 2015

Dedication

As adults we sometimes reflect back upon our childhood and those people, whether family, friends or neighbors, who personally gave us their time and attention, cared for us without limit, and sought to help us gain traction as we prepared for our own independent lives. Most often these were ordinary people who had enormous influence because they cared. We are indebted to them. I offer the thought that we should recognize and honor them today as they continue, through our reported memories, to encourage us and others to do likewise.

More specifically, I dedicate *784 Broadway* to the memory and work of Thomas M. Menino, who served as mayor of Boston for 20 years. Mayor Menino treated every child in the City of Boston as one of his own. You could observe the mutual love and respect when, surrounded by a group of school children, he would ask how they and their families were doing. He had a unique and genuine way of determining the health of the city's many neighborhoods and how well his administration was serving them. Tom Menino fought tirelessly to find the necessary resources to make sure Boston school children were not going hungry and had a safe place to go before and after school hours. Menino knew these children would be the backbone of Boston in 20 years, and he was preparing them for that role.

I pray that God remembers him as a mayor who, for his entire political career, freely spent his political capital – and often his personal health – to improve the lives of all Bostonians, especially those living on the margins of society.

Acknowledgement

My thanks to Henry Quinlan, Omni Publishing Company, for his willingness to team up again as I dared venture out of the fiction genre to write this remembrance. Critical to this effort reaching fruition is the guiding presence of editor Theresa Driscoll and her ability to encourage me to allow the child to speak but allow the reader to discern the conclusions. Her ability to bring order out of chaos at times also helped.

I view a book cover as a work of art that both introduces and contributes to the story. It has the power to immediately inform the prospective reader and help set the desired tone. Leonard Massiglia of LMA Communications has again done my cover. The cover photograph, which has been on my office wall for years, suffered from exposure. Len's talents allowed him to restore and fit the photo, which is very special to me, without reducing its character. It is a home run.

My three primary readers are repeats from *Necessary Assets*. Their time, effort, and input were again substantial. I would have quit early on had it not been for the contributions of Ron Gollobin, Ken O'Brien, and The Reverend Susan Baker-Borjeson. Their observations about *784 Broadway* help introduce this remembrance to prospective readers.

I had yet another editor. I asked my 15-year-old grandson, Liam Kaplan, to perform a technical edit of an advanced draft and to tell me whether a young adult would be interested in reading this book. I was impressed by the quality of his edits, his suggestions, and the reasons behind his views. Thank you, Liam.

My former FBI colleague, Art Ryall, and my two longest friends, Jim and Marie McCrohon, provided this author some much needed balance. I found it more difficult than I anticipated to write a remembrance about my own family. I also extend my thanks to

Connie Kastelnik, of CK Communication of Boston, for her help in exposing my writing to a wider audience and for pushing me out of my comfort zone when it comes to self-promotion.

I end with a special thanks to my bride, Merita Hopkins. I am beginning to realize how difficult one can be when pre-occupied with a writing project, even one that is enjoyable and embarked upon voluntarily. I return now to the world of fiction to continue the sequel to *Necessary Assets*.

Prologue

I spent many years as an FBI agent working two Italian organized crime groups, the American La Cosa Nostra and the Sicilian Mafia. After arresting the La Cosa Nostra leadership in Boston for a second time, one LCN leader said to me in an aside, after checking to see who might be listening, "The problem for us is you think like we do. How is that?"

We both smiled. I understood his backhanded compliment. He was right. I could think like them. I could and did turn that thinking into a strategic investigative advantage for the FBI. Like the bad chess player's offering, I sometimes saw and understood their move before it was completed. I was familiar both culturally and historically with their view of the world. He liked to bully. I liked to help people being bullied. The speaker erred in assuming he knew my ethnicity and cultural background based only on a last name. In *784 Broadway*, I describe my immigrant Italian heritage and the profound role this heritage played in setting my moral and personal compass guiding me from childhood into adulthood.

I invite you to visit this world I call Kingston as recalled through my stories and photographs. I invite you to remember those in your life that may have played a similar role.

The Deceptive Arrival

The air is crisp, cool, this early June morning and the dew has not yet been tamed by the morning sun. We have driven all night. We know what we want to do, what we will do. We slowly ride by 784 Broadway. With our heads forward, my brother and I look out of the corner of our eyes to see what is going on inside the greengrocer store at this address. We can't afford to have the two men inside alerted to our presence. The men are moving crates of produce around inside the store getting ready for the day's business.

Our intelligence tells us we have only a few moments to pull this off. Soon the local truck farmers will be coming by to deliver their produce. There could be witnesses. We don't want that.

"Pull around behind the store," my brother Danny tells the driver. The driver turns right off Broadway onto Albany Avenue, pulls in behind the greengrocer store and cuts the engine.

"Ok. Jim and I are going in together. We'll do it. You'll know when to follow us in." Heads in the car nod. "You ready Jim?"

I nod yes, but am not quite ready. I am still stiff from the drive. I have to give myself a short pep talk. I can't mess up. These men are good but we are going to get them this time.

"I'm ready," I tell Dan.

The driver lights a cigarette. He says nothing. He looks neutral.

We get out of the car, stretch, and saunter towards the entrance of 784 Broadway. We walk in the door full of confidence, like we own the place.

John Garbarino is wearing a white apron. His brother Gordon, wearing a red plaid shirt, is sorting through a box of oranges. They haven't recognized us yet. "Can I help you?" asks John.

"Yea," says my brother Dan, "I want a head of lettuce, a bunch of carrots, and a couple of red onions."

John Garbarino says nothing, takes a bag from the counter, puts in three red onions, and places them on the scale. He reaches for a head of lettuce and a bunch of carrots and puts them on the counter. I'm starting to go crazy. When is Dan going to do it?

"Give me two pounds of red plums," says Dan.

John Garbarino takes another bag, puts eight or so plums in it, weighs the bag, and puts it on the counter. Two pounds exactly. He never misses. I am keeping an eye on Gordon Garbarino as Dan and I had earlier agreed. I notice his hands are not moving as fast as before. He is holding the oranges more than actually sorting them. I think he is suspicious of us.

"Anything else?" asks John, but we know they are onto us for sure. Dan and I see John look at Gordon and give a slight nod. Gordon has a devilish smile and John's right hand moves behind his back. It's over.

John grabs my brother Dan in a bear hug. Gordon does the same with me. Dan and I are yelling "We fooled you! We fooled you! You didn't know it was us."

"Well of course," said John, "you have grown so much bigger since last summer we could never recognize you."

We are so happy and excited to see our great uncles John and Gordon Garbarino. I am eight years old and Dan is ten. We have driven with our parents, Joe and DeSales Ring, all night from Baltimore, Maryland to come to Kingston, New York on vacation.

Our baby brother Michael is three years old and still pretty much asleep when our parents enter the store and begin their own round of warm greetings.

***

Our arrival and the ensuing weeks for me can only be described as joyful. I can still feel my great uncles' bear hugs today. They are hugs of love, joy, and an affection that never diminished through the years. While John and Gordon were never prone to verbal discourses of affection, I remember how they treated us as children, and even what they said to other people in our presence.

Even today I can hear my great uncles saying, "This is my sister's son's boy." I can picture how they would stand a little straighter, and give a slight nod of pride in my direction. John and Gordon always made me feel like someone important when they did this. In fact, I know that to each of them, I was.

I want to tell you about this annual tradition, which starts at 784 Broadway, and how it positively influenced not only my childhood, but also my adult life.

First, Some Questions

Why did my Kingston family have such an extraordinary influence on my life? Their impact was substantial and not at all proportional to the limited time I spent in their presence.

How did a tiny greengrocer and fruit store at 784 Broadway operated by my great grandmother and two great uncles, all with limited education, ingrain in me ethical, economic, financial and business lessons that have lasted a lifetime?

How did my Uncle Bill, mayor of Kingston from 1943 to 1949, friend of Franklin Delano Roosevelt at Hyde Park, founder of a society that to this day trains disadvantaged adults for employment, and long-term board member of the Mother Cabrini Home for Girls, instill in me a recognition that a meaningful life always includes time set aside for public service?

Through a collage of stories told through my window as a child, a young adult, a father and FBI agent, I look back with pride and great love for these simple yet extraordinary people who taught me, by example, about life and how to comport myself when addressing its complex challenges.

As the harsh reality of aging took its toll on those I loved, I looked at my own children and wondered what kind of influence I was providing them. How effective was I in creating a loving value system within them that bore some resemblance to what I absorbed from my Kingston family, two generations distant from me?

Some History and Local Italian Truck Farmers

It is circa 1950. Kingston, New York, is located ninety-one miles north of New York City and fifty-nine miles south of Albany. Kingston is situated just east of the New York State Thruway with access to the Hudson River through the Rondout Creek. In 1777, Kingston was named the first capital of New York over the much larger and far more prosperous New York City, which was thought too vulnerable to a British military attack. In the end, the British easily reached Kingston and burned the city. This resulted in Albany being named the state capital, which it remains today, even though New York City is no longer under threat of attack by the British.

The greengrocer and fruit store bearing the name Joseph Garbarino has been located at 784 Broadway, at the corner of Albany Avenue, since about 1894. Etro Modica is an Italian American truck farmer who enters the store at six-thirty this fine summer's morning. I am James Ring from Baltimore, Maryland. I am spending some of my summer at the store with my father's bachelor uncles, my great uncles John and Gordon Garbarino.

As a truck farmer, Modica sells all he produces on his small farm adjacent to the New York State Thruway just outside of Kingston. His customers are the local Kingston produce stores. He delivers his fresh produce daily on his small flatbed green truck with wooden slat sides. John and Gordon buy produce from him and other truck farmers during the summer growing season because their produce is fresher and of higher quality than that of the local food distributor who obtains his produce from the New York City produce market. Perhaps even more important to John and Gordon is the fact that Modica and the other truck farmers are Italian. Modica is also a long-time family friend and part of a tight-knit community of Italian truck farmers earning a living doing something they love.

Modica murmurs "Morning" to John and Gordon with a slight Italian accent, hard to pick up since only one word was spoken. John and Gordon respond by nodding back to Modica in unison, uttering no words. You would think words were expensive?

As an eight year old, I get what could almost be detected as a slight nod from Modica. I return what I got.

In a much stronger voice, with his head tilted up toward an empty hole in the store ceiling (the store's winter stovepipe removed for the season), Modica says, "Morning Grama. Howa you today?" His Italian accent is now pronounced, as I knew it would be.

Next I hear the vigorous ring of a small porcelain tea bell. Assunta "Susie" Garbarino, known in our family simply as "Gram," the matriarch of our clan, has just acknowledged Modica's greeting with a solid ring of her tea bell.

Gram is eighty-eight years old, blind from glaucoma, but in fine health otherwise. She is still in bed. Her son John is too busy at the moment to go up to the family's second floor apartment over the store to help Gram up. That will wait until the early morning store chores have been completed, generally by seven-thirty.

Gram follows all the comings and goings in the store through the stovepipe hole. Those who know Gram and the family often raise their voice to pass along a greeting or to let her know some piece of their family news. The response is the same. A tea bell ring acknowledging message received and thank you. Despite her infirmities, Gram remains a participant in the social and business fabric at the fruit and vegetable store at 784 Broadway as she has since she and her husband Giuseppe opened the store in 1894.

Uncle John and Modica walk to the street where Modica has his truck parked. I follow. John views the produce Modica has for sale this morning. This time of year most produce is available daily: green beans, tomatoes, lettuce, peppers, cucumbers, radishes, scallions, blueberries and onions. Corn is eagerly awaited and appears the middle of July. John does not place an order with Modica ahead of time knowing Modica will show up each weekday morning at six-thirty. John selects the produce he needs for the day and Modica hands it to me from the bed of the truck to place on the ground outside the store.

"No raspberries today?" asks John.

"No," Modica responds. "Gotta no one to picka yesterday. Your boy wanna picka today?"

John looks in my direction and smiles. This is a game he and Modica play with me. Modica grows raspberries, strawberries and blueberries, and offers to pay me a quarter for each quart of berries picked. When he first asked me about picking last year, the quarter sounded pretty good but I declined. John said I made a good choice as berry picking could be back-breaking work. The truth was I loved being in the store with John and Gordon. There was nothing else I wanted more.

After Modica completes his business with John, he is off to another day of picking the produce that will be placed on his flatbed truck late this afternoon for delivery early tomorrow morning. Modica is followed shortly by "Joe on Pearl Street." Joe is another Italian truck farmer who to my knowledge was never located on Pearl Street.

Why he bore that name remains a mystery to me. I never asked. Once you were introduced and given the person's name that was his name forever. You didn't question history. A long-time family friend named "Torino" was from the town of that same name in northern Italy. All the years I knew him, everyone called him "Torino." His son was called "Frankie Torino." You can imagine my surprise when I learned, well into my adulthood, Torino was not his real name. It was, I discovered, common for someone to be known by the name of the town or "paese" in Italy from which they emigrated. When you said Torino, everyone knew who you were talking about so there was no problem. It worked.

Some of the truck farmers grew more fruit than vegetables. Apples and peaches were big sellers by the pound, peck, and one-half or full bushel. Some local pears and cherries would also appear and, later in the season, watermelons. Fruits not grown in the region, such as bananas and citrus, had to be purchased from the local food distributor linked to the larger New York City produce market.

Other truck farmers stopped by the store to sell what they had left on their trucks or, if they had already sold all their produce, for a brief social call. John always tried to spread his purchases out among the truck farmers so that no one was left out. Even if he had all the peaches he could store for one day, John would ask a farmer to bring six half-bushels the next day in order to give that farmer a sale. This was my first experience witnessing how honorably these men conducted business with each other. If the peas were not holding up, the farmer would say so. If it was going to take four days for the peaches to ripen, then that is what John was told. Even as I child, I knew this was the way people should treat each other in business. Their mutual respect was obvious. These truck farmers supported each other. If Modica needed more beans for an immediate delivery, he might get them from "Joe on Pearl Street." They made it work for each other.

John has been running the store with his mother, Gram, since John's father and store founder, Giuseppe "Joseph" Garbarino, died in 1913 at age fifty-two. John was twenty-three at the time. Then, his younger brother Gordon would help at the store when he was not employed elsewhere. Now, from years of experience, John knows what Modica and the other truck farmers will bring to market for sale day to day and week to week.

The Beginnings of My Family in America

So why was I visiting this tiny store in Kingston, New York, every summer and loving every minute of my time there? What is it about my family in Kingston that makes me want to honor them now by writing their story?

In 1950 I knew few details of the Garbarino family history. They did not talk about their past or where they came from, and I did not know enough to ask. Most of what I now know has been pieced together over the years, augmented by research. I knew Gram was my great grandmother. She and her husband had come from Italy, where both were born. As a child, I never thought to ask what city, town or region they called home. I never asked what drove their parents to leave Italy and seek a new life in America. I didn't even know what an Italian was. By the time I realized what a profound influence these people had on my life, and was interested in learning more, those who knew had died. When I questioned my mother in later years, her response was to ask, "Why do you want to know that stuff?" She thought it didn't matter.

As I found out too late, it did matter to me. The Garbarinos are such a part of my being that learning about them was learning more about me. But people who immigrated during this time period wanted to quickly assimilate into the American life and put their past behind them. Perhaps talking about their native country and those left behind was just too painful. Best to forget and move on.

My great grandmother, my "Gram," Assunta "Susie" Garbarino, was born March 18, 1862, and died May 28, 1959, at age ninety-seven. Piecing together bits of data, I believe Gram's father was named Antonio and her mother Louisa. Her place of birth is listed in census records only as Italy, with no region or town cited. Gram immigrated to the United States in 1881 at age nineteen, arriving in New York City.

Assunta married Giuseppe "Joseph" Garbarino (age twenty-one) in a civil ceremony before New York City Alderman Charles G. Marto on June 27, 1882. Their certificate of marriage cites it was witnessed by Antonio Garbarino, father of the bride, and Giacomo Garbarino, father of the groom. This marriage certificate makes me wonder why two Italian Catholic families, new to the country, would have their children marry in a civil ceremony. They both had the same last name, as did their fathers. Could it be they were first cousins prohibited from marrying in the Catholic Church? Were they from the same village in Italy? At least it is certain that Gram was a newlywed to Joseph Garbarino and they were both now living in New York City in June of 1882.

My Great Grandfather, Giuseppe "Joseph" Garbarino, was born in Italy in 1861 and immigrated to the US in 1870 with his parents, Giacomo Garbarino and Pasqualina Garbarino. He was likely accompanied by his sister Rose. Thereafter, Giacomo and Pasqualina Garbarino operated a fruit store on Church Street in lower Manhattan for twenty years, from roughly 1870 to 1890. They relocated to Kingston shortly after 1890.

Within two years of their marriage, Joseph and Gram moved from New York City to Kingston and began operating a fruit and confection store. My great grandfather Joseph Garbarino first appears as a Kingston resident when listed in the Kingston City Directory of 1884. When Gram died in 1959, she was described as a seventy-five year resident of Kingston, indicating also that she arrived in 1884. Their first store was located at 3 Wall Street; the second was located at 333 Wall Street, and the third at 784 Broadway. It would appear that by 1890, Joseph's parents, Giacomo and Pasqualina, and his sister Rose, had left New York City and followed him to Kingston.

By 1894, my great grandparents were operating their own fruit and vegetable store at 784 Broadway, at the corner of Albany Avenue. At the same time, Joseph Garbarino's sister Rose and her husband, John Gotelli, were operating their fruit and vegetable store a few blocks north at 333 Wall Street. Later, as the widow of Giacomo, Pasqualina owned the building at 333 Wall Street from which her family ran their store.

I seemed destined to never find out from what Italian "paese" or town Gram's family had emigrated. All the shipping manifests from the time contained limited data about each passenger. Most entries consist of a last name, first initial, and the country of origin. The birthplace is always listed as just Italy. Then there came a clue!

I recalled that for years an old man named Tony periodically came into the store, said very little, hung around, and then would be gone. He didn't seem to like children. When he did speak, he spoke gruffly. I could not understand him through his thick Italian accent. He scared me. Finally I asked Gordon who he was. Gordon said Tony was a "paesan" (from the same village or paese) of Gram. According to Gordon, the Garbarinos sort of looked after Tony as he had no family locally.

Many years later, in some Garbarino family papers, I found a United States of America Declaration of Intention filed by one Tony Giacchero in the Fairfield County, Connecticut, Superior Court in September 1918. In this document Tony renounced forever his allegiance to the King of Italy, Victor Emmanuel III. The document states that Tony was born February 22, 1873, in Sassello, Italy. He came to the United States through Havre, France, on the vessel

Gascogne. This I knew was a port, a route, and a ship that brought many northern Italians to the US. I now believe that Sassello, Italy, is where both Gram and Joseph's families emigrated from. It also fits with the information I had about their coming from the "Genoa area." Today Sassello remains a small village, home to just 999 families, located just west of Genoa.

I knew there were other relatives of the Kingston Garbarinos in New York City, but that ends my knowledge on the subject. I never knew any names nor knew of any family visits during my early years. I know that when opportunities in New York City seemed limited, young couples would sail up the Hudson River seeking their future.

Gram and Giuseppe – Their Family at 784 Broadway Expands

In 1888, Gram gave birth in Kingston to their first child, Elizabeth Josephine Garbarino, known by all as "Lizzy." Two years later their first son, John, was born. Mary Rose (Aunt Mamie) was born in 1894. The fourth and last child was James Gordon, born in 1904, twenty-two years into their marriage. Gordon was doted on by his sister Lizzy, who was sixteen when Gordon was born. They remained extremely close over their lifetimes.

My passport into the Garbarino family of Kingston was my father, Joseph Edward Ring, born in 1916, in Brooklyn, New York.

While the Garbarino family was settling into Kingston in the late 1880s, my paternal great grandfather Jeremiah Ring, born in Ireland in 1854, came to Kingston to work as a blacksmith for the railroad. His wife Anna, born in 1859 in New York City, bore him two sons, Joseph Henry Ring (my grandfather) in 1889, and his brother Leo Francis Ring in 1893.

In May of 1890, Jeremiah bought a newly built residence at 8 Clinton Avenue in Kingston, which later becomes an important part of my Kingston experience.

My grandparents, Elizabeth Josephine "Lizzy" Garbarino and Joseph Henry Ring, met in Kingston where they both grew up and went to school. A Kingston *Daily Freeman* (KDF) news clipping from June 23, 1905, states Elizabeth was an outstanding student at the Kingston Academy, winning a Modern Language Honor (at age seventeen) upon graduation in 1905. Lizzy and Joseph married October 15, 1912. About the time of their marriage, Joseph secured a job with American Telephone and Telegraph Company in New York City. They moved from Kingston to Brooklyn, New York, where my father, Joseph E. Ring, was born in 1916. His brother, John "Jack" Ring, was born four years later.

Six months after my grandparent's marriage, my great grandfather Giuseppe died. At age twenty-three, John Garbarino stepped in to run the family greengrocer business with Gram. John continued to reside with his mother, running the store, until she died in 1959.

In August of 1918, Gram's second daughter, Mary Rose, known to me as Aunt Mamie, married William F. Edelmuth at St. Joseph's Church in Kingston. Eight years later they purchased 8 Clinton Avenue (the Jeremiah Ring home.)

On a number of census forms, before the purchase of 8 Clinton Avenue, Aunt Mamie and Uncle Bill are recorded as living at 784 Broadway, in the small apartment over the store. Uncle Bill was a tobacco salesman and was often on the road during the week, but when he was home the quarters must have been very close. Uncle Bill served in the US Navy during WW I aboard the USS Adams, which probably resulted in Aunt Mamie living at home over the store while he was away.

So how did the residence at 8 Clinton Avenue come to be purchased by Aunt Mamie and Uncle Bill?

When Jeremiah Ring died intestate in 1926, my grandfather and grandmother, along with Leo Ring and his wife, inherited the Jeremiah Ring family home at 8 Clinton Avenue. They in turn immediately sold the house at 8 Clinton Avenue to Aunt Mamie and Uncle Bill, who occupied the house from 1926 until Aunt Mamie died in 1976.

Life sent my grandfather and his brother in different directions. My grandfather was transferred by AT&T from New York City to Baltimore. The family had to move. Grandfather Ring, along with his wife Lizzy and sons Joseph (age ten) and Jack (age eight), moved to 5526 Selma Avenue, Halethorpe, Baltimore, Maryland.

My grandfather's brother, Leo Francis Ring, also married after school and left Kingston when he obtained a job with Western Union Telegraph Company in New York City. He resided in the Corona neighborhood, in the borough of Queens.

My father, Joseph Edward Ring, attended Catonsville High School and later Johns Hopkins University. He remained in Maryland when my grandparents and his brother Jack moved to Chicago when my grandfather was transferred by AT&T. My father was in love and in college. In 1937, he married Ann DeSales Knecht of Baltimore, Maryland.

At graduation, the Depression was still on. My father got a job climbing telephone poles for the Chesapeake and Potomac Telephone Company, despite having an electrical engineering degree. He was glad to have any job at that point in time.

While we are here, I will mention that in 1940 my parents bought the Selma Avenue house in Baltimore from my grandparents, who were still living in Chicago. Selma Avenue would be my childhood home until age twelve, when my family moved to Ellicott City, Maryland.

Elizabeth "Lizzy" Garbarino

I have a clear memory as a young child standing in the kitchen of our home on Selma Avenue in Baltimore, Maryland. I am almost five years old and my brother Danny is almost seven. My mother is telling us that we are leaving immediately with Dad and Uncle Jack to drive to Kingston. I recall thinking this was strange because it was not the time of year for our trip to Kingston. It was not summer. Mom was not coming but Uncle Jack was? This was different.

I vividly recall today, and can clearly picture in my mind, being led shortly thereafter into the main bedroom apartment over the store at 784 Broadway. The room was dark, quiet, and adults were standing around the bed.

I felt like I was in church but could not see the altar as I was surrounded by adults. Suddenly a path to the bed seemed to clear magically. I was propelled forward by unknown hands. There was a lady lying in the bed. She was beautiful. She wore a white gown and the bed had brilliant white linens with lace. The lady had a beautiful, warm smile when she looked at us. Everyone was so quiet. The woman was peaceful.

I now know the woman was my grandmother Elizabeth "Lizzy" Garbarino Ring. Lizzy died April 8, 1947. I was two months shy of

my fifth birthday when this bedroom scene took place. Yet I remember it as clearly as if it were yesterday. Why? This is the only memory I have of Lizzy. She was dying from breast cancer. We were being presented to her for the last time. Can you imagine, I am not five years old and have this detailed a memory?

My grandmother Lizzy came alive to me over the years through the words of her brothers and sister. They greatly regretted, as did I think Lizzy, that she was unable to live with her family in Kingston. She visited often, especially after they built the old Camp in the late 1920s. Her sons Joseph (my father) and Uncle Jack would use the Camp as their summer meeting place for all the families, children, and friends. These gatherings served as the basis for the joy of Camp.

Lizzy also comes alive to me now as I look at the photos of her Camp visits. I recall the great affection that John, Gordon, Mamie, Uncle Bill, and most of all Gram, had in their voices when they spoke of Lizzy. My mother told me that after Lizzy was diagnosed with breast cancer her doctors treated her with radiation, which at that time was still experimental. The radiation burned her badly and was very painful. Uncle Gordon, who was only nine years old when Lizzy married and moved away, then drove to Chicago, put Lizzy in his car and drove her back to Kingston where he personally cared for her until she died. These actions are a testament to how Lizzy and her family always stayed close, despite their physical separation. It is also the testament of a family that knew how to love its members.

Whenever I asked Gordon about my grandfather, of whom I knew little, he was either evasive or silent. It did not take a genius to figure out there was no great bond of affection between Joseph Henry Ring and the Garbarinos of Kingston. However, to the Garbarino family credit, I never heard anyone speak an ill word against my grandfather. Demonstrative love may have skipped a brother-in-law. However, any lack of love was certainly made up when it came to the progeny, my father, his brother Jack, and their children.

Driving to Kingston

How did Joe, DeSales (my mother, known to all as Dee), my two brothers and I get to Kingston from our Selma Avenue home? When my brothers and I were young we mostly tackled the 350-mile journey at night. No one wanted to waste any time getting to Kingston, so as soon as Dad got home from his job with the Chesapeake & Potomac Telephone Company the car was immediately packed and we were ready to go. An example of a nighttime drive to Kingston is this trip in 1950 when I was eight years old, Dan was ten, and baby brother Mike was three.

Once out of our immediate neighborhood (about two blocks away), I had no idea where we were. I knew enough about how long the trip took so I didn't immediately start asking how long before we arrived in Kingston. Riding at night way past my bedtime was always an adventure. Thrilling at first, but soon enough my brothers and I would always succumb to sleep.

On this particular night we woke up because the car became uncomfortably hot as we waited in a line of cars for the ferry (no bridges yet) across the Delaware River. We could elect to have more fresh air in the car by rolling down the windows, but we knew we would be swarmed by mosquitoes. We rolled down the windows anyway, and got the fresh air and the mosquitoes. Next we changed our vote and closed the windows, which gave us mosquitoes and no fresh air. This was one lesson we learned over and over again each year.

Riding any ferry across a river at night was an exciting adventure for an eight year old. The smell of the water, the rocking of the boat, and seeing all the trucks and cars packed together in the ship's hold was a memorable experience for me each year. There was no Delaware Memorial Bridge or New Jersey Turnpike at this time. We traveled Route 1 North to the Delaware River ferry, and onto the back roads of Pennsylvania and New Jersey before entering New York State.

Dad had driven this route so often it was like a short ride for him. When we got a little older we traveled more often by daylight. If doing a daytime drive, there was a particular tree in Pennsylvania that I looked for and recognized. The center of the tree had a circular hole cut out to allow the passage of electric and telephone lines. I was always impressed that this tree was not cut down because it was in the way. Instead, the hole transformed the tree into a work of art, at least enough to impress this young boy. Come to think of it, my brothers were never that impressed with my tree. As soon as I saw my tree I knew we were taking a route through Amish country and would watch for the farmers driving their horse and buggies on the same roads we drove. To a kid from the city, this felt like the Wild West.

The daytime drives usually took longer thanks to ongoing construction projects slowing traffic and causing delays. The New Jersey Turnpike and New York State Thruway were under construction for so long it seemed like forever. The reason I remember this part so well is because Uncle Bill purchased three dump trucks, which he in turn leased to contractors working the New York Thruway construction project. He sent us pictures of the trucks, each with a nameplate on its hood. One truck was named Dan; the second was Jim; and the third was Mike. He named a truck after each of us! For the next few years, any time I saw a dump truck I looked to see if my name was on the front of the hood. Talk about a way to keep a young kid busy on a long drive!

I had the address of 784 Broadway, Kingston, New York, memorized before my own home address. The store front faced Broadway, the town's major thoroughfare. The rear faced Albany Avenue or Route 9 W, the old route to the Catskills and points north from New York City. Albany Avenue also laid claim to many fine residences of the Kingston wealthy to whom we regularly delivered fresh produce.

A Camp Overview

After our long night drive in 1950, it was early morning when we arrived at the store. After Dan and I try to fool John and Gordon upon our arrival, Dad, Mom and Mike enter the store and chaos reigns for a little while longer. John and Gordon say they were fooled by us. It is not true, of course, but there is always hope we will fool them next year. The conversation in the store is unstructured and allows for more than one person to speak at the same time. This seeming chaos allows all of us to catch up on family news in short order.

After the arrival and morning visit, followed by a big noon-time meal, John and Gordon pack up my parent's car with food before they set out on the ten mile drive to "Camp." Camp was known to the Post Office as RFD 1, West Hurley, New York. During my early childhood years, I was deemed "too young" to stay at the store and went off to stay at Camp with my parents and Mike. Dan was a little older and got to stay at the store before I did with Gram, John and Gordon.

Over the course of our vacation, there was constant driving back and forth between the store and Camp, depending upon fishing schedules, errands, and whatever work Gordon convinced my father was needed to repair or improve the Camp. My father, with his electrical engineering background, did a lot of construction and electrical work at Camp while on vacation. It was a labor of love for him at a place he loved.

After the morning store orders were delivered to the customers and our daily shopping route directed by Aunt Mamie was completed, Aunt Mamie would accompany us to the store for the mid-day meal and to visit with and tend to her mother's personal needs. After lunch we drove her home. Then either Gordon or John, along with Gram plus one of us, would drive to Camp for a light afternoon of work and a visit.

In the mid-1950s, a second, "new" Camp, was constructed next to the original, "old" Camp. The old Camp (built in 1928) was tiny. It had two bedrooms with only enough room for a bed in each; one small, heated main room; and a tiny kitchen with a booth. The original outhouse was still located next to the garage. The outside, uncovered hand pump for the well water, augmented by two huge brass rain barrels, was still in use when I was a child. The old Camp had a front, screened-in porch (great for summertime sleeping and rainy days) overlooking the Ashokan Reservoir and the foothills of the Catskill Mountains. There was a second, but smaller, screened-in porch in the rear.

The new Camp was constructed over several years. It was a walkthrough (railroad style) ranch house where John, Gordon and Gram intended to retire whenever that time came. This was as far as their retirement planning went. They were always happy as things were.

Camp Life in the 1930s and 1940s

Camp was a lively and popular gathering spot for friends and family in the 1930s and 1940s, and tents were set up in the backyard to accommodate anyone who wished to visit. I recall my mother telling me that after she and Dad were married in 1937, they honeymooned at the Camp. Unfortunately, it was in July and at the height of summer activities. Mom and Dad did get their own tent but not much privacy, as they were surrounded by other larger tents in the already crowded backyard.

The fact that my parents chose to travel to Kingston for their honeymoon and spend their time with Dad's grandmother, uncles and aunts is something I can understand, having experienced Kingston as a child. Much of the attraction to Camp was the draw of nature and the chance to live in community with family and friends in a way we did not do the rest of the year. Today we would understand that better if we talked about leaving city life, with its attendant work and family obligations, to get back and live more closely with nature, visiting with people for whom we have the greatest love and affection. This is something I inherited both physically and emotionally from Kingston.

Interestingly, my brother Dan and his wife Nancy spent their honeymoon at Camp, as did my younger brother Michael and his wife Jackie. While being newlyweds without a lot of money could have accounted for some of the Camp's honeymoon attraction, I think it was more that my brothers wanted to insure their wives became part of the Kingston culture. To my knowledge, none of them was required to sleep in tents with other guests in the middle of the backyard.

Photos from the earlier period show a time when family and friends were able to gather, share, participate and bond with each other in a way that perhaps could not be duplicated after World War II. Our family in Kingston seemed to get through the Great Depression intact and still in business. The Depression had its negative effects but it reinforced the idea that they could better survive this downturn if they were willing to support each other, share, and be willing to do with less, as long as they had the basics. It was probably a good thing that John and Gordon, along with their friends, were practiced in the art of fishing and hunting. They consumed much of what nature had to offer, without being overly concerned with the legal definition of fishing or hunting seasons. Hunting and fishing were less about sport, and more about making sure family and friends had healthy food on the table.

There were people of all ages at Camp during the summer. As the war progressed, more women held jobs previously occupied only by men, now off to war. This changed many aspects of their daily lives. Some of the younger, married women now liked to smoke cigarettes and drink beer or whisky like the men. Mom told me that during this time Gram would excuse herself and retire early for the evening while the others remained outside under the night sky, sitting before the crackling outdoor fireplace. Gram knew the ladies were reluctant to smoke or drink in front of her, as this was not her custom or the way she was brought up. She would not grant overt approval to the ladies sharing cigarettes or drinks with the men, but she would not offer any resistance or interfere. Mom always said Gram was the most informed person in Camp when it came to gossip. She would go to bed early and listen to every conversation until the entourage disbanded for the evening. In a quiet only shared with nature, voices carried well.

Gram is another who taught by example. It could involve action or inaction. As I discovered with John and Gordon, it is what they did, not what they said, that oftentimes most impressed. My mother was saying the same thing about Gram. She had her opinions but was not opinionated.

My First Fishing Adventure

When I was younger and required to stay at Camp with my parents, my father often arose early in the morning to go fishing at first light in the Ashokan Reservoir, situated directly in front of and one-half mile below the Camp. The reservoir was constructed during the early 1900s by African American and Italian laborers in a valley flooded out after its completion in 1912. The Ashokan Reservoir was, and is presently, a major drinking water gathering and storage facility for the City of New York. From anywhere on the Camp property we could look down the hill and out onto the reservoir and the rising Catskill Mountains on the far side. As a young child, I would sit out on a stone wall at the quarry across from the front porch door at the old Camp and just look at this scene. Even as a child, I was mesmerized by this view.

When Dad returned from fishing, I would just be getting up. I watched him clean the fish. I cannot say I thought it a pleasant experience, but it is what you had to do if you wanted to eat the fish just caught. To this day I can smell the freshly caught fish Mom cooked quickly over high heat in a frying pan. I like to fish today. I still don't like to clean the fish, but since I like to eat them…

I recall my first fishing experience with Dad and Gordon on the shores of the Ashokan Reservoir. Across Route 28A, the small country road in front of the Camp, was the reservoir fence built of concrete posts securing a firm, hard wire fence. There were several cut-outs built at various points along the road to permit foot-passage through the fence. One was across the road from the Camp. You did not have to climb the fence; you walked through the cut-out. You could only be on reservoir property if you had a fishing license and were going fishing.

To a child, the half-mile walk downhill to the water seemed much longer. I learned it was hard to carry a fishing pole through the woods without constantly snagging the line in the trees. When we arrived at the water's edge on this first trip for me, Dad put a worm (actually a night crawler) on my hook and gave me a few in my own tin can mixed with dirt and damp leaves. From that point forward I was expected to bait my own hook, following his example. Dad and Gordon walked the edge of the water casting their worms at places that looked good for fishing. The one thing I was told by Dad and Gordon early on in my fishing career was that you had to be quiet to catch fish. I would make no noise.

Dad and Gordon had moved along the shore away from me in search of fish, which seemed in short supply this day. I was just about to follow them. Being unable to cast a fishing line yet, I just dropped the line with the hook and the worm in the clear water at my feet. I could see the rocks under the water and my worm wriggling around on my hook. Dad motioned for me to follow him and Gordon as they moved on. Just then I saw a large bass swim up to my hook and conduct an inspection of my worm. I had never seen a real live bass fish in the water before. I was going to catch a fish! I remained perfectly still. I would make no sound to scare away the fish before he decided to consume my worm and consequentially the hook! I was in fishing heaven watching this bass and preparing for the strike. I waited, waited, waited, and the fish kept being most curious about my worm but did nothing more.

Next I could see my Dad motioning me more firmly to pick up my line and follow them. I wanted to tell him I had a huge fish ready to attack my worm, but I didn't want to make any noise and scare the fish away. Quiet was what I was supposed to be when fishing. What a standoff. I finally knew I had to move along. I tried to bring the hook in slowly, hoping that would incentivize the fish to attack. No such luck. I brought the line in and ran after Gordon and my father. When I got to them they were seriously fishing another section of the shoreline. I knew I was not supposed to talk and I didn't. It was not until we were back in Camp, fishless, that I managed to tell them my story of the curious bass and my worm.

My memory is that this great fishing adventure story did not merit more than a curious look and a couple of grunts from them, individually and collectively. I was disappointed. I wanted them to be as excited as I was. Perhaps they were and I just couldn't tell?

An Outside Tour of the Old Camp

The old Camp had a screen door off the side of the front porch that exited to a driveway. It was the most used entrance, the door closest to the outdoor social area, and offered the best view of the Ashokan Reservoir. Across this driveway was a bluestone wall about three feet high that marked the edge of an old quarry. From this and other area quarries, bluestone was mined to build the beautiful stone walls around the reservoir. Even the sidewalks of Kingston's tree lined streets, as well as those of other cities, were constructed using similar bluestone.

In later years, when maintenance of these remarkable sidewalks and stone walls became a cost issue, the walls were torn down and replaced with metal guardrails. Macadam replaced the bluestone sidewalks. The now "scrap" bluestone from the torn down walls and sidewalks was, I am told, sold by the contractors in a somewhat political manner generating huge profits for themselves.

I almost cried when, as an adult, I first noted what they were doing. I complained vigorously to John and Gordon who could only silently shake their heads. For a child to love these bluestone walls and sidewalks, you know they had to be something very special. I felt as if the barbarian hoards had ravaged the area and plundered treasures they did not even understand. These walls were gone forever. I viewed the whole process both then and now as a desecration.

But now I shall step-down from my soapbox and continue the tour.

The quarry was where we used to dump our trash. When the pile got high, we set it on fire. Non-burnable material was taken to a dump a few miles down the road.

The quarry was also the place where I learned to shoot a gun. Gordon would tie a tin can on a string and lower it over the side at the far end. We would stand up by the stone wall next to the old Camp and fire at the tin can with a single shot .22 caliber rifle. They also had a World War II .30 caliber M-1 carbine semi-automatic, which to this day is one of the neatest guns I have ever handled. All gun handling and instruction was done under the strict supervision of Gordon and my father. It was here that we learned to respect a gun as well as the basic safety rules for handling a gun. It was not overdone. It was a special treat. In this strong hunting environment, where guns were common in households, you wanted to teach children proper gun-handling skills.

Okay, I admit the cherry bombs were another story! Around the Fourth of July, Gordon would get some cherry bombs and we would go to the quarry. Gordon placed a cherry bomb under a tin can with the fuse sticking out the bottom. He lit the fuse with his ever present Zippo lighter and stood back. The cherry bomb would explode with a loud bang sending the tin can many feet into the air. We could each select a tin can and Gordon would place and light the cherry bomb under the can we selected. We could see whose tin can was sent the highest in the air. Somehow, I don't recall my mother ever choosing to participate or even witness these antics.

Past the quarry next to the driveway was a huge outdoor wood fireplace and cooking grill. It was used a lot during the summer when larger crowds were on hand. This area was a social gathering spot that provided shade during a hot day. At night people would sit around the outdoor fireplace to socialize, with the fireplace smoke doing an excellent job keeping the mosquitoes at bay.

Past the fireplace, on the back edge of the property and alongside the garage, was the one-seater outhouse. Remember I said the Camp water was supplied from a hand pump? It was located outside the kitchen and was not under any cover. This meant there was no electric water pump and, thus, no indoor plumbing. The hand pump and brass rain barrels provided drinking water and water to wash. The existence of an outhouse is next in this logical progression where no indoor plumbing is available.

There was a smell to this outhouse which today I still recall and not fondly. I was told that is where you had to go, there was no other choice. When you protested to Mom or Dad, they would remind you firmly the outhouse is where they went. This was probably the first time in my life, which I can recall, where I had to control my feelings and physical reactions in order to do something necessary. Perhaps this was my first serious dealing with adversity where I just had to put mind over matter. It was, of course, not the last time.

I mentioned the garage located next to the outhouse. Does a garage have a smell? Oh yes, one of its own. This was a small, free-standing wooden garage with barn type doors in front with glass panels roughly painted black. There was a smaller side door which we used for entry and exit. I never saw the front doors open. The garage floor was dirt but roughly covered in places with what appeared to be portions of left over macadam dumped in place and roughly spread out. This garage was a treasure trove where I spent hours just looking things over.

The first smell that comes to mind from the garage is wet canvas. It took me a while to figure out what exactly I smelled. Crawling around in the garage, I found the loft or overhead storage in the rafters full of canvas tents, chairs and awnings. It appeared to be excess military gear. There was enough canvas to set up a small city or quarter an army platoon. Everything needed for summer outdoors was stored in the loft. Excess military gear was easy to come by at this point in time. Some of this gear can be seen in the photographs of the period.

There were boxes of tools I had never seen before. There were axes and hatchets that I would never be allowed to touch at home. Here I had no restrictions. It was assumed I would know how to handle this treasure hunt.

There were brass tank fire extinguishers that strapped to your back and expended water using a slide hand pump attached to a hose that connected to the bottom of the tank. Put ten gallons of water in this and hike to the fire in the woods. It was a very heavy load. No wonder they preferred to use shovels and dirt to put out fires. These backpack extinguishers did serve as excellent devices to water flowers. The only other choice for plant watering was to carry buckets of water after filling them from the hand pump or the rain barrels.

Being curious about why the garage windows were painted black, I asked Gordon why this was done. I don't recall his answer exactly, but I do remember thinking I never really got an answer to what I thought was a simple question. Eventually I put it together.

There were some wild rumors that my uncles may have participated in deer hunting during a period of time not officially sanctioned for such activity by the State of New York. Translated, they would hunt deer out of season, or so rumor had it. Normally, a recently-slain deer is gutted and left to hang a few days in cold weather to season the meat. During hunting season, neighbors would have their deer hanging in the front yard so anyone going by could admire their hunting prowess. Out of season this is not a good thing to advertise. Hence, one can hang a deer in the cold garage with painted windows and closed doors until it reaches meat maturity. After this is done a few times, a wooden garage with somewhat dirt floors tends to develop a unique smell.

Should, in your absence, a local official choose to visit your locked garage, he would be unable to see anything inside the garage through the painted windows. When I finally figured out this whole scenario, I realized the game wardens and my uncles were not always on the same team when it came to deer hunting. More on this subject as we progress.

The Smells of Camp and the Store

It was in Kingston as a young child I first realized my sense of smell was more than just useful in telling Mom that my Brother Michael's diaper needed changing. I think to a child a smell is regarded as either good or bad, and we react accordingly. In Kingston, I realized that you could note a smell, categorize it by place or event, and store it in a memory bank for later use.

When age required me to stay at the Camp with my parents, the day was my own. I was reasonably free to explore my surroundings at my own pace. I was never bored. In bad weather I could sit inside the screened-in front porch and read, look at the reservoir and the mountains, follow all the local wildlife Camp had to offer, and all from this perch.

To this day the smell of pine trees, which surrounded the entire Camp area, immediately reminds me of Camp. We did not have any pine trees where we lived in Maryland so the scent of pine trees around Camp was delightful to me. This scent created a special signal in my brain active even today. When I walk the woods, as I often do, and smell a pine tree, I immediately have a picture of Camp in my mind.

Often the smell of summer flowers in the garden will trigger my memory to return to the scene of John's circular flower garden located between the old and the new Camps.

An equally influential memory generated by smell is that of fresh fruit and vegetables. Place these in a confined space overnight, as done in the store at 784 Broadway, with no refrigeration, and you have a unique olfactory event. It reminds me of the store, without fail. When you got up in the morning and came down to open the store, you would instantly note a delightful aroma. The aroma of ripening fruits and vegetables can only be experienced in such an environment. Likewise if coming in late at night after the store had been closed for several hours, the effect was the same.

There is a greengrocer where I live in Boston's Italian North End. I shop there regularly and the smell I just described is ever present. I have told the store owner of my childhood experience and response to this particular earthy fruit and vegetable aroma. He smiled. He understood what I am talking about.

My First Overnight Visit

My mother still declined to let me join my older brother Dan and stay at the store with John, Gordon and Gram. They would beg my mother to let me come but she was reluctant to do so at my yet tender age, feeling perhaps I would not have the necessary supervision. Still looking for a way to break the ice, my mother responded to Aunt Mamie and Uncle Bill's invitation for me to stay overnight at their house at 8 Clinton Avenue. This, thought my wise mother, gave me a little more supervision and perhaps I was ready for that step. I recall this first stay in great detail because Aunt Mamie teased me about it for many years thereafter.

The story begins late afternoon at the store. Gordon was to drive Aunt Mamie and me to her house so we could prepare dinner for Uncle Bill and have it ready when he got home from work. After being mayor of Kingston, I don't think Uncle Bill ever held a regular job but he seemed to keep business hours and was always meeting with someone to do something. After Uncle Bill arrived home, we had a delightful dinner. Both Aunt Mamie and Uncle Bill answered all my questions at the dinner table patiently. I always thought them a treasure trove of information.

After dinner was cleared, Uncle Bill sat in his favorite chair, lit his pipe, and read the newspaper. I loved the smell of his pipe (I took after him and smoked one for many years). Aunt Mamie bustled in the kitchen cleaning up. I sat there with nothing to do and no one seemed to notice. They were not used to having a young child around.

There was a TV but it was not turned on until later in the evening, and then only to watch shows I didn't understand. Uncle Bill and Aunt Mamie did not watch Howdy Doody. There were no cartoons. I continued to sit and look around, trying not to offend on my first visit. As it got toward bedtime, this really strange feeling came over me which I find hard to describe. I was with people I loved and yet felt this sense of unease. Apparently at that point, according to Aunt Mamie's official version of this night, I announced my desire to be immediately returned forthwith to "my people" at Camp. I did not wish to sleepover.

What good sports they were. Without hesitation they called my mother to report this development. No one made any effort to change my mind. We all got into the car and Uncle Bill drove me ten miles to Camp so that I could sleep with "my people."

Not long after, I successfully completed my first stay-over with Aunt Mamie and Uncle Bill. Later on I realized the effort they expended to make me happy. It enabled me to realize I could stay with them without anxiety. It was clear I had a case of being homesick. Their response to me was so uniquely positive; I was cured of that disease forever.

Summer Swimming

As a young boy, I never knew what a "swimming hole" was. In Maryland, a few times over the summer, our family would go to a sandy beach located on one of the area rivers that flow into the renowned natural habitat known as the Chesapeake Bay. There were numerous day camps along these rivers with man-made sandy beaches for families to visit. It was also a time before these areas were built up and before the rivers were polluted by human development. This beach trip did not require one to drive down to the Chesapeake Bay itself or to take the ferry across the bay to the Eastern Shore and drive more hours to reach Ocean City, Maryland. This was a trip for people who could not visit the ocean for a whole week. If we had a week, we would always go to Kingston. I don't think I ever visited Ocean City until I graduated high school.

When it was announced at Camp we were going to the swimming hole, we all piled into cars and drove a few miles down the road from Camp, past the spillway area of the Ashokan Reservoir, to where a stream ran out of the south side in what was a well-shaded forest. We emptied out of the cars now parked on the side of this narrow country lane and walked a few steps to a stream, which had a pool about knee deep. It was not like the beach on a river at home. The adults, I finally noticed, were not wearing bathing suits. They rolled up pant legs and sat on a rock shaded by overhanging trees. I looked around. How could I jump into the water here? How could I swim in this somewhat limited and confined area? I had learned by this time in my life, not always well practiced I must add, to observe first and not ask a lot of questions. So I waited and observed. Everyone picked out a rock, sat down and put their legs in the running water. They splashed the cool water on their face and arms. The pool was large enough for people to laze about if they were willing to sit on rocks in moving water.

After doing my reconnaissance, I waded into the pool and found out immediately why it needed to be no bigger. One could not easily remain in the pool covered by water and breathe at the same time. This was a cold mountain stream that was instant air conditioning on a very hot day. I had never felt water this cold before. It was not long before I sought a patch of full, warm sunshine in which to stand.

The adults continued their conversation. Everyone enjoyed the shade and cooler air from the stream's flow. It was a lazy, near swim but more relaxing. The younger ones explored the stream's edge up and down. What neat things to be found. Maybe these were real Indian arrowheads? I wondered if the Indians, when they lived in this area, came here to bathe?

There was another nearby swimming hole called the gorge, which I later visited with Uncle Bill. When the water level was high, excess water from the Ashokan Reservoir would flow over a fixed dam (a spillway) and down a rocky gorge carved out by nature from huge boulders the size of houses. Out in the full sun at the bottom of one small part of this gorge, water gathered in a shallow pool before passing on through a narrow gap and going farther downstream. It was hot on these rocks in the full sun. It was difficult to climb down into the pool to enter the water and return back to an area where it was level enough to sit or lay on your towel. It was an interesting place to visit but not a place to hang around for an afternoon.

When I reflect on these swimming holes now, I am struck by the simplicity of what we did. Don a bathing suit, grab a towel, and drive a couple of miles up a country road. It was not an all-day affair that required the planning skills of an MBA. It was a refreshing moment of familial congeniality that required little and offered a lot. An hour or so at a swimming hole, followed possibly with an ice cream cone on the way back; it did not get any better.

Uncle Bill and Aunt Mamie had a Camp of their own located ten minutes from their home at 8 Clinton Avenue. I mentioned earlier that Kingston is bordered on one side by the Rondout Creek. This creek flows into the tidal Hudson River and its water level is impacted by tidal Hudson up to Uncle Bill's Camp. There were high and low tides which Uncle Bill countered by building a floating dock.

Their Camp sat directly on the Rondout Creek, in an area called Eddyville. It had a small bay that ran from the river behind the cabin. It was another place where I sometimes swam in the summer. Besides the cabin and the floating dock, they had a first-class fixed dock, with a sleek wooden outboard motorboat as well as a twenty-eight-foot cabin cruiser. I spent less time at Uncle Bill's Camp then I did at the Garbarino Camp in West Hurley. More on Eddyville later.

More Fishing Adventures

As mentioned earlier, we sometimes walked from the Camp down to the shore of the reservoir to fish. However, as the water warmed during the summer months, the fish took off for deeper, cooler water. Fishing from shore was less successful and a boat was needed to get to the deeper water. The reservoir limited the places where one could launch a rowboat (no motors allowed) and they were located in places inconvenient to fish. There was an answer for us.

Just down the road from the Camp was an old restaurant, painted white with a screened-in front porch, a large and beautiful wooden bar, and a huge kitchen with the biggest black stove I had ever seen. It was owned and operated by Torino, our long-time family friend, whom I mentioned earlier. A portion of the restaurant building also served as his home. Torino was famous for his steaks and outdoor oyster roasts, the latter of which were held in the late spring or fall as long as he could drive to New York City and purchase the most delicious oysters available.

It seems that somewhere along the way, Torino got permission to keep three wooden rowboats in the reservoir cove located down a path across the street from his restaurant and home. He kept these for his customers, friends and referred special people. We fit all three categories so we had use of a rowboat whenever needed.

I went fishing many times with my father and Gordon in these rowboats, generally in late afternoon or early evening. We would get a set of oars from Torino, march down the path, slide a heavy wooden row boat from the shore into the water, and off we would row. More correctly said, my father would row while Gordon and I watched. To a young boy, this was great adventure.

To step into a wooden rowboat that rocked because you did not know how to balance yourself; getting your tennis shoes wet from small puddles of water resulting from boat leakage, rain, or both; learning to bail water from the rowboat with a tin can; watching the oars being placed in their locks; feeling the pull of the oars as the boat started to glide across the water; hearing the slap of the water against the boat hull as movement started; these were all adventures that never grew boring for me as a child. While unsophisticated and mundane to many, I am sure this activity set a tone for and established the value of adventure in my life. It has never left me.

When rowboat fishing in the reservoir, we used live bait most of the time. Black bugs called Dobson, as I recall, were an inch-and-a-half long with pincers on their heads. These were purchased from a bait shop. Night crawlers (big worms) were found under piles of wet leaves, in soft dirt, under trees, and were mostly gathered at night using flashlights. Getting the bait on the hook was another adventure. Putting a big juicy night crawler on a hook required a young boy to fight being squeamish. My father and Gordon were even more amused to watch me put a Dobson on a hook, as I tried to avoid the bug's pincers. I never thought of whining to them about this part of fishing, which I did not like. I think whatever I said would fall on deaf ears. You want to fish, bait your own hook.

Sometimes when Dad was rowing us back into the cove after an evening's fishing, Uncle Gordon would put on the end of his line a floating lure known as a bass plug. He would allow it to drag behind the boat. The plug imitates a fish in distress. I was not sure what he was doing until I saw a fish slam into the plug thinking he had a great meal. Instead, because of the plug, we did.

We generally fished until dark. We walked back up the trail to Torino's in the dark without problem. We knew the half-mile trail well. Once back, we would sit at the bar (yep, me included). Dad would have a beer and Gordon a whisky, brand named PM, and I had a coke in the bottle. Torino's restaurant was not a hot spot with lots of people coming and going. In fact, it was well past its prime but still a favorite of locals who had shared good times with Torino for over fifty years. We were often the only ones in the place.

Here I was sitting at the bar with my father, a great uncle, and an old man who spoke with an Italian accent so strong that often I did not understand him. I would nod my head as if I did, but I didn't. I was never asked to repeat or explain what he said so I found just going along and keeping my mouth shut worked just fine. I was not sent outside to "play" or told how to occupy myself. It was up to me. Sit with us if you like. Whatever their conversation, it never seemed like much to me. What was important to me is that I was welcome to be with them.

Over time I lost track of Torino. As an adult, I came to visit Gordon one time at Camp to find that Tornio's wife had passed away. Torino sold his restaurant and home. A new family purchased the property and converted the restaurant side of the building back into a home area, making it one large residence. Even in later years, when I drove by Torino's, it still looked the same. The screened-in front porch looked just as inviting, and I still looked in the parking lot hoping to see Gordon's car parked there. Even knowing that time had passed, the habit remained and my heart wanted it to be like it was before, but would never be again.

Finally Store Approved

It happened the summer I was nine years old. We arrived at the store and again failed to fool John and Gordon as to who we were. John and Gordon asked my parents, as they did each and every summer, to let me stay with them at the store. This year my parents agreed. It was their considered opinion that I was old enough, at age nine, to be of invaluable assistance to John and Gordon in the store. For the first time I would be on my own. This time when they drove off to Camp, I was the only child staying at the store. It was my turn at last! I cannot say that my stomach didn't do a few flip flops or that I didn't have some apprehension, but the time had come and I wanted to do it.

The apartment over the store was a cozy place to me as a child. It was simple, efficient, and to me very loving and comfortable. Sometimes, I try to picture life in the Garbarino apartment above the store at the turn of the century. When I think back to Joseph, Gram, and their four small children, along with Gram's sister, Pasqualina Gotelli, living with them now and again, crowded is the word that comes to mind. With no bathroom and a shared toilet with the next door neighbors, I add the word uncomfortable to the word crowded.

Anyone visiting the Garbarino clan, prior to the old Camp being built in 1928, had to crowd into this tiny apartment. How did they do it? In later years, when Lizzy and her husband Joseph, along with their children, my father and his brother Jack, returned to Lizzy's home for a visit from Brooklyn, the situation must have been even more demanding. Add to that, Aunt Mamie and Uncle Bill were living there, according to census records, from their marriage in 1918 to 1926 when they bought 8 Clinton Avenue.

From our experience in the Italian, North End section of Boston, my wife and I know Italian immigrant families in cities spent much of their time in the streets, which served as their living rooms except in the worst weather. Men had religious clubs to which they belonged and where they could congregate to socialize. Women leaned out the windows to communicate with neighbors. When warmer weather arrived, the women sat out on the front steps to talk with each other. Children played in the streets until it was time to go to bed. Basically, the apartment served as a place to sleep and a place to eat. Personal hygiene was attended to in the local bathhouses.

This way of life under these physical conditions would not be acceptable to many of us today. We have experienced a life that offers us more material comforts. However, I have on many occasions heard some of my older Boston North End neighbors speak fondly of this immigrant lifestyle. It was a village lifestyle and there was community. The eyes and ears of the neighborhood served as a deterrent to bad behavior by children. Even if you did the act a few streets away, your parents were likely to be quickly informed. You also ran the risk that one of your neighbors cared enough about you to administer some on the scene "correction" to deter a re-occurrence. This community perspective helped me appreciate the crowded life in the apartment above the store many years before.

The Apartment above the Store

At the rear of the store were two steps up, which led through a narrow hall to a full set of steep, narrow stairs. At the top of these stairs was a hallway that led to four rooms. The first was the slanted floor "parlor" with no furniture and which I never saw used except as a place to put my suitcase. It looked as if the original building had a slanted roof that was covered over and made into a room that really had no usable space. In crowded times I have no doubt the room was in full use with sleeping bodies, slanted floor or not. The second was the bedroom of John and Gram. The third was the kitchen, dining and family social area. The fourth room was actually a continuation of the hallway leading to a step down with a half-door, which was the entrance to the toilet shared with the family next door. There was just enough room on one side to have a double bed pushed up tight against the wall. This was Gordon's "room." When staying at the store, I slept with Gordon in this bed or on a "daybed" located in the kitchen, depending on whether my brother Dan was with me. A few more words about the use of this space will round out the picture of the apartment.

Gram's bedroom, shared with John, is the same one I recall being led into as a five year old to visit my grandmother, Lizzy, before she died. I can recall that windows on the Broadway side let in sunlight and made this bedroom a cheery space. Present was a potty chair for Gram, tended to by John. I had never seen one before and had to ask John what it was. He gave me a straightforward, factual response. There was a wardrobe for clothes and a rocking chair I would occupy on those evenings when John asked me to keep Gram company for a while. (I have lovingly restored this old rocking chair, which now sits in my Boston bedroom. It is too small and delicate for a modern, physically larger, adult to use, but I love it. It is a prized possession that helps connect the historical thread.)

Upon entering the kitchen, there was a cold water sink to the right, a daybed to the left, and straight ahead a large black wood cooking stove, long ago converted to gas. It had white porcelain knobs to control the gas and a shelf above the cooking area. The kitchen had two windows facing Broadway which, like Gram's bedroom, provided generous daylight and warmth. Between the two windows was a mirrored stand where Gordon and John shaved.

A bulky, darkly-wooded bureau stood on the wall opposite the stove and contained all the dining implements, china and glasses they possessed. Completing the kitchen furniture was a matching round table with four matching chairs, accompanied by a few extra chairs matching nothing else in the room.

A Comfortable Living Space

Now that you are familiar with my physical accommodations at 784 Broadway, I want to explain why I think it was a comfortable home. Not everyone thought or felt the way I did. I remember my mother questioning me to determine if I really wanted to stay at the store with John and Gordon. It was only later that I understood what she was really asking. She was gently noting the lack of conveniences to which I was accustomed in our home on Selma Avenue. I didn't wash myself or my clothes at a cold-water sink, nor share a toilet with strangers. I told her I was completely happy staying at the store with John and Gordon, and I was.

As is the tradition with many families of varying cultural backgrounds living in apartments, the kitchen table was ground zero and the absolute center of family activity. Owing mostly to a lack of space, this was the gathering spot for the immediate family, neighbors, friends and visiting relatives. It was the early version of today's popular "open floor" concept plan, combining living room, family room and kitchen. Nearby was an active coffee pot, espresso maker or perhaps a tea kettle. This also describes the second floor kitchen at 784 Broadway.

John prepared the first food of the day after the store was opened, the produce placed outside, and the initial transactions with the local truck farmers completed. Gordon would take over the store so John could fix Gram's breakfast. She drank strong espresso coffee with lots of milk, which I later learned was a cafe latte. Into this she dipped a hard biscuit, or "biscotti." John fixed her a varied breakfast menu of oatmeal, scrambled eggs, sliced Italian bread toasted, and bacon done well. The aroma of the bacon early in the morning is still one of my favorite olfactory memories.

After John and Gram had their breakfast, Gordon and I would go upstairs for some coffee, milk, cereal, or scrambled eggs cooked in olive oil. Gordon was not interested in bacon, as that was for Gram. I still enjoyed the lingering smell. I could have asked for bacon, and I am sure it would have been given, but that was just not the way it was.

The breakfast meal was also my first chance to experience a loaf of unsliced Italian bread purchased from a local Italian bakery, which was a new experience for me. I was used to the white sandwich bread that had overtaken the ever-expanding supermarket bread shelves. Italian breads were purchased only from an Italian bakery. There were several in Kingston, but none that I can remember at home. Having to slice the bread allowed me to make the toast slices as thick as I wanted.

We used an old electric toaster that required the user to open the toaster door while toasting was in progress and the electric elements were red hot, and turn the slice of bread over to toast the second side. The heating coils could only toast one side of the bread slice at a time. I got to the point, after eating many pieces of burned toast, where I could toast both sides of the bread evenly using this "manual" toaster. What a wonderful smell the fresh Italian bread had as it toasted. Even today I use the same Italian loaves, which I slice but put in a toaster oven. I have not seen a "Kingston" toaster since my days at 784 Broadway.

Breakfast was also my introduction to coffee. Gordon fixed coffee for me, although I did note that my cup had more warm milk added than did his. In the center of the round kitchen table was a sugar bowl with a silver lid that folded to close the glass container when not in use. It had a slot where the spoon rested. You may see one in use even today in an old-fashioned diner. However, progress today has dictated these sugar bowls be discarded in favor of the prepackaged sugar packets. I am sure someone did numerous health and efficiency studies to insure this was the best course of action and recommended it to every local health department. It also destroyed the option of asking a neighbor at the counter to pass the sugar bowl, which was often a good way to start a conversation while waiting for your breakfast.

The Daily Store Routine

Monday through Saturday, the routine of store life remained much the same. John was always the first up by 6 a.m. and was shortly down in the store carrying out all the produce stored inside overnight. He met with the truck farmers, made his purchases, and had the store ready for customers by seven-thirty. Examining all the bins to remove any rotting fruit or vegetables, trimming greens, and sorting through the berry boxes, were all part of the morning routine.

Unlike John, and more like Gordon, I was not a morning child. The cool morning fresh air just made me roll over and remain curled up in the blankets. John never went out for the evening, after store closing time. He went to bed early. Gordon went out mostly every night to visit various watering holes frequented by his friends, or to visit his girlfriend, or sometimes just go for a ride to the reservoir area to see where the deer were at dusk. Often he would invite me to go with him and I might not get home with him until 11 p.m. or sometimes later. Sometimes in the evening Gordon offered to cook a meal for a friend busy running a bar. Sometimes he cooked a special meal, such as lobster, while relaxing at his girlfriend's house. Gordon took pleasure in cooking for others. I do also. I think I know where I picked up that trait.

Some mornings I would feel uncomfortable laying in a warm bed knowing John was working alone to get the store set up. I would get up and go down to the store and start helping him. He never asked me to help him. But, I began to value this part of the day spent alone with John working with him in the cool early mornings. I could see he was also happy that I would willingly do this on my own.

By 8 a.m., the store phone would start ringing. FE (federal) 8-1347 was the store phone number. Calling in their fruit and produce orders for the day were the cooks who ran the kitchens for the wealthy families, as well as the homemakers who were regular customers. There were few two-car families, so our daily store deliveries were a necessity for those at home without a car.

We would fill the telephone orders placing the produce items in paper bags, which in turn we placed in wooden boxes. We loaded the boxes onto boards placed over the back of the store's red, early 1940s, International pickup truck Gordon drove to deliver the orders. In gold letters, on each truck door, appeared the name J. Garbarino, along with the 784 Broadway address and phone number. There was no delivery charge. Home delivery benefitted both the business and the customers.

What was really special was that I got to ride on the back of the truck, in the open air, all over Kingston and on the way to Camp. I sat on the boards laid across the truck bed, along with the orders. I could talk to Gordon as he drove. What an adventure! I am sure my mother worried but Gordon was a great driver and never went over twenty miles per hour. I also learned to be a responsible rider, which was part of the deal. If I messed up, I would be back inside, riding on the front seat with Gordon. I don't recall that ever happening. It was a great way to get to know the town. I felt like I was on top of the world when I was riding on the back of the truck.

When we arrived at a customer's house, I would take the order to the back door, which usually led directly into the kitchen. Before entering I would knock and call out "Garbarino delivery." Many of the people we served watched me grow up over the years. Often they would step outside and tell Gordon how big I had gotten and how nice it was to see me again this year. Some of these clients knew my father when he delivered orders with Gordon a generation earlier, just like I was doing now. I thought this was neat. It made me proud. I was part of something. I was beginning to understand being part of a larger community.

Learning about People

It was not easy for me at first to make these store deliveries to the kitchens of these large homes. I was not used to interacting with adults who were not aunts or uncles. The customers were mostly strangers. They generally knew who I was but I really did not know them. After carrying the order in, I would wait while the lady (generally it was) checked the order. I would answer any questions I could or go back to the truck and ask Gordon. As I look back now, it was excellent training for a young person to develop the basic principles of human interaction. I learned to look the other person in the eye while speaking in a clear, audible voice. Not easy for any naturally shy young child to learn. John or Gordon would say as they did, "this is my sister's son's boy." I would say John and Gordon were my great uncles, but that did not seem to be enough. I would tell the person I was doing what my father did as a child before me, helping John and Gordon in the store, and that I lived in Baltimore and was visiting for the summer.

People were mostly very nice. Since this was also a time of year when produce was plentiful and "canning" was done, I often carried in half bushels of peaches, tomatoes, beans, peas, or anything else that was being "put over" in quantity for later winter consumption. The first time a lady put a coin in my hand when I finished making a delivery, I didn't know what to do or say. I went back to the truck and showed Gordon the coin and told him what happened. He explained that the person was giving me a "tip" for my service of carrying some heavy containers, and that I could keep the money. After this experience I noted that the nicer the customer was to me, the more likely they were to thank me with a coin. Infrequently, but sometimes, a customer would not even bother to look at me. The most I might get after I said hello was a "put it there," with a nod toward a counter or tabletop. I was beginning to learn about people.

I began to ask Gordon questions about his experiences with customers or what happened when he delivered when I left to go home. Gordon did not take tips. It was part of their store service. Some people, whom he knew for years as customers and members of the community, might send a hello back to Gram. Others, whom he had known equally as long, treated him as a servant allowed in the house only long enough to deliver the produce. I did not like the idea of anyone treating Gordon or John with a lack of respect. I don't think they held this type of person in any esteem, no matter how rich they were. On the other hand, they did not complain when someone looked down their nose at them. I have always been glad for this experience at an early age. It taught me to be more observant of other people. It also caused me to think of the type of person I wanted to be, and how I should treat others. Even today, I don't suffer lightly those who belittle or bully another.

At times there were customers at the store who enjoyed being critical of the produce, complaining about the price being charged, and who thought nothing of damaging a piece of fruit by squeezing it to see if it was ripe enough. They never wanted that squeezed item in their bag, but I always made an effort, with quick hands, to make sure it went into their bag. I also began to observe that unhappy people seemed to want to share that "gift." John and Gordon exhibited patience with these people. They were there to sell produce and this was part of the business of dealing with customers. They made little of it. I have always had more difficulty in this area and some noted that I scowled at customers who were rude to my uncles. Some people even claim I do that today to those who look down their noses at others. I was unable to emulate John and Gordon's "business" attitude when dealing with these difficult customers.

Learning to Cook

After breakfast Gordon and I delivered the orders. Next we picked up Aunt Mamie from 8 Clinton Avenue. She would immediately direct us to two or three stores she pre-selected in order to do our family food shopping for the day. She had read all the market sales advertised in the daily paper and we shopped strictly and obediently according to the sales identified to us by Aunt Mamie. In the kitchen above the store we had a small, European style refrigerator that held little. We generally shopped each day and only for the items needed for that day's consumption. Very little was wasted shopping this way. We continued the old tradition of having the principal meal of the day at noontime. I continued during the daily shopping run to ride on the back of the truck, through the tree-lined streets feeling free as a bird, while assisting in these arduous shopping duties.

Sometimes I was delegated by Aunt Mamie to go into the meat market and personally conduct the meat purchase. I assumed that Aunt Mamie was giving me detailed instructions for me to repeat exactly to the butcher to avoid any error. After telling me what meat and how much to purchase, Aunt Mamie also said to "make sure the butcher doesn't put his thumb on the scale." I was not sure what this meant so I just told the butcher exactly what Mamie said, figuring the butcher would know what she meant. When I later mentioned to Gordon that I did not think the butcher liked me after I gave him Aunt Mamie's specific instruction, Gordon laughed. It was not like he explained to me what I had done. You figured it out for yourself after a while. Perhaps it was another form of the Socratic Method?

After we completed the daily shopping run and returned to the store, we briefed John on our purchases, discussed the menu for the noon meal, and then Gordon, Aunt Mamie and I headed upstairs. Aunt Mamie was an outstanding cook in her own right, but at 784 Broadway she spent her time addressing the personal needs of her mother, making her comfortable, happy, and feeling loved. She also got a chance to have someone cook for her for a change.

I was on standby to assist Gordon, our daily cook, in whatever chores I was assigned. It was here with Gordon that I started to learn cooking basics. Gordon was considered by family and friends to be an excellent cook, so I had a great teacher. Boys in the 1950s, in my economic and social strata, were not needed nor required to be in the kitchen for training. This was the mother's province. Most mothers at the time did not work outside the home and would be listed on the census forms as homemakers. How many college women at the time were slotted into Home Economics study? Children showed up at the table for supper with the father and, if cooking was to be learned, it would be daughters who were instructed by their mother. Boys learning to prep a meal, cook, and wash dishes were concepts not in vogue.

My mother encouraged my learning to cook with Gordon. My mother also made sure I could perform basic sewing repairs. She did not want her sons to be helpless in these and other handy domestic skills. My mother grew up in a household of eight children during the Great Depression where everyone had to help growing, storing, and cooking food for the entire family. Her mother died when she, the oldest, was only nineteen and the youngest was five. Everyone had to pitch in and help to keep things going.

I think my mother liked what I was learning from life at the store. It was not long after I exhibited my joy in learning to cook that mother added to my knowledge base by teaching me how our home washing machine worked. I could now wash and iron (beginners level only) my own khakis for school. I was being raised as a Renaissance man, capable of being self-sufficient.

Like any apprentice, my initial assignments with Gordon were not lofty. I was told what pots and frying pans to get out, saving Gordon from having to bend over. They had blackened, tin frying pans of various sizes. I had not seen any pans like these before. They were light enough for me to handle easily and responded quickly to the gas flame. They were just very basic, functional, workable pans Gordon used for years. But there was no pan or flame for me at the start.

"Would you peel the potatoes?"

"Sure Gordon, how do I do that?"

Gordon showed me, starting with a potato peeler and later using a small paring knife. I also learned the proper technique for husking corn as well as shelling fresh peas or preparing green beans to be cooked. I was introduced to fava beans, which we never had at home but are a great favorite with Italian families when accompanied by Pecorino Romano cheese and a glass of red wine. I hadn't been acquainted with red (Italian) onions, which then came attached to a stalk by braiding their papery stems together. In the store these were sought after as sweet and mild onions. Sometimes I made sandwiches with Italian bread, mayonnaise, and these red onions along with freshly sliced and recently picked tomatoes sprinkled with salt and pepper.

Gordon also introduced me to garlic. My mother used garlic at home, I am told, but since I didn't labor in her kitchen I didn't know how or when she used it. Gordon showed me how to peel a clove from a garlic head and either crush the garlic in a press, chop it, or slice it thinly. It all depended on what we were cooking and what the role the garlic was to play in the intended dish.

Whenever there was olive oil placed in the frying pan (we didn't say sauté at the time), it was most often followed by an introduction of garlic in one of the above forms to flavor the oil. Gordon was always very careful about having the flame just right at this stage. Later I understood he was trying to keep the garlic from burning, as this ruins the subtle garlic flavor. I was only observing this action, as I was busy with my food prep chores.

This was my first introduction from Gordon on the use of olive oil for cooking. Gordon used it liberally. After a while it became second nature to me, even before deciding what I would cook, to already have my hand on a tin of Italian, green, first cold pressed olive oil. No one in this family had any heart problems.

When boiling water, a little salt was added to encourage the water to boil faster and sometimes a little olive oil for a thin coating on the vegetables or pasta being cooked. During the summer months we enjoyed everything grown locally. Garden fresh vegetables were picked in the afternoon, delivered to the store the next morning by a truck farmer, and were cooked and on our table by noontime.

One of my favorite dishes was fresh string beans blanched for just a moment and then sautéed in a little olive oil and garlic. I also came to like plain, boiled, fresh carrots. When they are just picked they are so sweet, tasting almost like a crunchy candy. I was taught not to overcook these foods in order to enjoy their freshness.

Understand, this was not a cooking class put on by Gordon. He never instructed me step-by-step. He let me watch. He would answer my questions but more often just wanted me to figure it out. I only realized this later in life when I found myself over-explaining a cooking point to my grandchildren. You could see their eyelids start to descend as they became bored with an explanation containing far more information than they needed or wanted to know. Children like to figure things out on their own. They sometimes learn best by osmosis. It took me a long time to learn this.

A hamburger is just a hamburger. Right? I don't think so. When we went to the butcher shop to buy ground beef, chunks of beef were cut from a larger piece of aged meat hanging on a hook in the cooler. These chunks were put into a meat grinder by the butcher and ground up. An hour later the ground beef was in our frying pan, being cooked with olive oil, thin slices of garlic and some salt. It was better than any steak. Hamburger, containing just the right amount of fat, accompanied by fresh corn on the cob dressed with butter, salt and pepper, along with garlic green beans or carrots lightly boiled, is still one of my favorite dinners.

I learned about veal cutlets and chops. I learned about cooking pork chops with vinegar and peppers. I learned about cooking chicken parts in a frying pan. Fresh caught bass, trout, pike (very bony), and various types of pan fish graced our table. Some we caught, others were brought to us by friends who shared with us their bounty after a good day fishing. Game birds were also a favorite. However, deer meat in all forms (steaks, chops, ribs, and ground) did not appear on the table until cold weather set in.

During the hot summer months we sometimes went at night to a muddy creek on the outskirts of Kingston. Gordon borrowed a flat-bottom row boat for us to "gig" frogs. What this entailed was having a car battery in the boat to which we could attach a powerful light. We would poll along the creek banks shining the light onto the shoreline looking for bull frogs. The light would freeze them. A long bamboo pole with a multiple barbed spear on the end would be used to capture or "gig" the frog, which would then be placed in a burlap bag. At the end of the frog hunt, we would take the burlap bag back to the store and clean the frogs in the upstairs sink. It was the frog legs that were the delicacy and they would be the feature attraction at the next noon meal.

The Cowboy Influence

As a young child growing up in Baltimore, I was accustomed to receiving an allowance from my parents of one quarter paid each Saturday afternoon, just before the start of the afternoon double-feature movie in the theater just down the street. These were the days of cowboy movies. Roy Rogers, Hopalong Cassidy, Gene Autry, The Lone Ranger, would all teach my generation great moral lessons. If you stole cattle or robbed the stagecoach, you went to jail. If you killed, you would be caught. If you were mean, you would get your comeuppance. If you lied, people would not like or respect you. Twenty cents would get me into the movie. That left me a nickel for a pack of candy. Necco wafers would last a long time as would gummy spearmint squares. However, I still have a love for Jujyfruits, savored one at a time to make them last.

No matter how many fights the hero got into, his cowboy hat remained neat, clean, and his clothes were never dirtied, rumpled, or stained. His horse and saddle were equally neat. You could always tell the bad guys before a word was spoken. He had a mean look, was unshaven, dirty looking, and did not smile a lot. He seemed to do a lot of spitting. He might even be so bad as to be rude to a woman or a horse!

At the end of the movie I walked home feeling like all was right in the world. Good always triumphed over evil. Our hero remained just that at the end of the movie. My friends and I wanted to emulate the hero and incorporate his thinking and behavior into our own.

Across the street from my house was a wooded area with the very busy Route 1, which ran north to the City of Baltimore or south to Washington, D.C., just on the other side of these woods. Beyond Route 1, there were multiple railroad tracks that served much of the north-south train traffic. This little patch of woods was the Wild West for me and my playmates. We all possessed some varied assortment of cowboy gear, usually pieces acquired for a birthday present, Christmas, or even an Easter gift. But the big deal was our cap guns and having a good supply of caps. We entered these woods packing loaded cap guns, looking to cure any injustice found within this wooded patch. Finding none, we had to use our imaginations to create some injustice and draft one of our group to play the role of the bad guy. No one wanted this role. Often it was necessary to find a mate out of ammunition (no caps) and offer them a few rolls of caps to assume this dubious role for a few hours.

"I got you!"

"No you missed!"

"I didn't miss. You're dead."

'Well maybe you nicked me but I could still shoot and I got you first."

This was of course the start of my learning the art of negotiation. We developed skills that could be very useful to those engaged in Mideast diplomacy today. These outings could last an entire day. Often we brought our grub (peanut butter and jelly sandwiches) to enjoy on the trail.

I digressed with the above only to set the stage for the reader to understand the importance of the cowboy life to an impressionable young child who had never touched a horse or a cow.

Would You Like to Ride a Horse?

It was probably not hard for Uncle Bill to get the drift that I was a fan of the great cowboy stars of the time. One day he came by the store and asked, "Jimmy, would you like to ride a horse?" I was stunned, quickly recovered, and agreed this was a great idea. In a very short period of time I had many visions of what this trip might be. I thought Uncle Bill was going to take me on a cattle drive, ride the dusty trail, maybe even right a few wrongs along the way. A child's imagination can create many expectations that would astound the logic of an adult.

We drove outside of Kingston to an area just west of the Thruway, still generally under construction and where many of the local truck farmers had their fields. Uncle Bill turned into and parked in an area with a wooden fence corral, some out buildings, and a larger corral where big and small horses were nonchalantly grazing. We went into a barn. I saw my first genuine leather saddle. I touched it. It was so smooth and had the most delicious odor. I studied the saddle horn, the stirrups, the cinch belts, and then spotted a bull whip hanging on a post. I stood there mouth open, wide-eyed, taking it all in. This was real cowboy! Uncle Bill had been off to the side speaking to a man. They stopped talking and the man we were visiting came over and took down the bull whip from the wall. He showed me how to snap it, and then let me try. Just to hold it was an unbelievable thrill.

We went outside to the open corral surrounded by a circular wooden fence. I watched the man saddle one of the small horses (later I discovered it was called a pony). He turned and asked "Would you like to take a ride?" The smile on my face and huge, affirmative nod answered his question.

I tried to put my foot in the stirrup but it was too high up. The man got a portable step box and put it alongside the pony so I could mount on my own. It would have been embarrassing to have to be lifted onto the saddle. I thought the man would open the gate so I could ride this horse through the farm land that surrounded us. My hopes were too high. He handed me the reins, but led me around the corral in circles. I was still in heaven. After I completed a lengthy and wonderful "horse" ride, I was allowed to explore all of the barn and surrounding area even where the horse lived. I loved the different smells of each area and was a most contented child when it was time to leave. I now knew what it was like to ride a "horse." I could tell my mates back home about this great adventure. Uncle Bill did something for a child that day that remains indelibly etched in my chamber of wonderful memories.

Uncle Bill would buy me new sneakers every year when I was in Kingston. He, as in the past, took me to his friend who ran a shoe store in Rondout, located down near the river of the same name. On the way there this particular year, I may have mentioned in the car that I could use a pair of cowboy boots. I think the response I got was "we'll see." Wow, it wasn't no. There was hope! A pair of real cowboy boots!

We got the sneakers. I said nothing about the cowboy boots in the store. I did look around but did not see any on display. In the car on the way back I mentioned the cowboy boots again to Uncle Bill by saying I didn't see any in the store. Uncle Bill said he would check with his friend someday about the availability of cowboy boots. Now, there is no way any reasonable person could even infer some type of commitment on the part of Uncle Bill to what I was thinking. However, when I left that summer to go home I concluded in my own mind that Uncle Bill never said no, and that he would check with his friend to get me the cowboy boots. To that conclusion I added another. Uncle Bill would not wait a whole year for me to come back to Kingston; he would ship the boots to me at home.

So for the remainder of the summer, anytime a delivery truck came down Selma Avenue, I would hop on my bike to follow it to see if it dropped off a box at my house. The boots never came. I went back to school. Somewhere around Christmas I imagined, out of whole cloth of course, that Uncle Bill would probably send me the cowboy boots for Christmas. That never happened, either. I never told anyone about my "expectation" of receiving a pair of cowboy boots from Uncle Bill. It was not considered polite to expect or lobby directly for a gift.

An Important Question – Where Do the Whiskers Go?

When I described the small apartment above the store, I mentioned the mirrored stand set up between the two kitchen windows facing Broadway. This was where John and Gordon shaved. They would heat some water in a pan on the stove and then bring it to this table where they kept their shaving mug, brush and razor. They were modernized in that they had abandoned the straight razor in favor of the safety razor. However, as was often the tradition or habit of the time, men often shaved every other day. While watching Gordon shaving one day, I asked him where the whiskers went after the razor crossed his face, leaving his skin smooth. Gordon showed me how they ended up in the pan of warm water as he rinsed his razor.

I remember this conversation with Gordon as if it happened yesterday. Why? I don't know. There are many learning experiences from Kingston, even meaningless ones like this, which remain front and center in my memory bank. How many of us have these simple, childhood memories of rather insignificant events that, it seems, will never be erased from our minds. It took me a long time to realize it was the little things I did or said to my children, and later my grandchildren, that were indelibly imprinted in their memory banks.

This thought makes me nervous. I don't think I have been as patient as my Kingston family members were.

I must also report that years later, after my father passed away, I found he had John's shaving mug, with his name painted on it, along with his brush. No one else wanted it. To the trash pile? No way. I wanted it. It now sits on a shelf in my bathroom next to one of my shaving brushes.

I am told shaving brushes and soap mugs for men these days are making a comeback. I am ahead of the curve on this one. I have used a shaving mug and brush every day for many years. I am afraid to delve psychologically into the background of this habit!

Learning about Charitable Giving

Sometimes the local Benedictine Hospital would call and place an order for multiple cases of lettuce, oranges, carrots, or whatever they needed. This was a larger than normal order for the store so we would drive to the local Kingston produce distributor to buy what was needed to fulfill the Benedictine order. This produce would be marked up in price to create a profit for the store and delivered immediately. John and Gordon purchased from the distributor for bulk orders or when the truck farmers ceased to have fresh produce at the end of the local growing season.

The first time I experienced a walk-in refrigeration unit was at the Benedictine Hospital when I carried the produce into it. Another experience I would not get back in Baltimore. After a while, I wondered why the hospital would call J. Garbarino & Son when they could deal directly with the distributor, as did John and Gordon. More than once, the distributor's truck was making a larger delivery to the hospital at the same time as we were making a small one. I asked Gordon why the hospital didn't just order everything from the distributor.

Gordon had a habit of not always answering my questions. At times he would grunt to acknowledge he heard the question. Sometimes he would answer, sometimes not. It was just his way.

Sometime later I realized that John donated cash regularly to this hospital. Perhaps not a lot, but it was always something. It finally dawned on me that the hospital ordered a small portion of their produce needs from the store because John supported their mission, and that of the Sisters who ran the hospital, and they in turn wanted to support him. I later asked Gordon if this was the case and he told me I was right. He said little else but perhaps enough to infer that it was a losing proposition for the store but it was John's decision to make.

I later learned from a number of less-than-direct conversations with John that he was a regular donor to a number of charities. He was of the philosophy that the Garbarinos had in abundance and he was willing to give a little of what they had to the many in need. From time to time over the years, I would pick up comments from more than one person who said they would like to have just what John gave away each year. John would have me believe he was only doing a little. The comments from others led me to believe he was doing a lot.

It took me well into my adult years to understand John's charitable activity. As I mentioned, besides the checks, John would regularly provide bags of produce to families in need. Any produce that might soon be marginal for sale always found a useful home.

This was the beginning of my education about sharing what we have with those who have less. I was learning by example and not by philosophical discussion. I was learning that when it comes to charity, the left hand should never know what the right hand is doing. If you do something for others, do it quietly and without notice. You don't have to explain yourself or expound on your philosophy, just do it. Others with eyes and ears will learn from your example, but only if their heart is in the right place.

This was also the beginning of my business and personal financial education. John, Gordon, and for that matter Aunt Mamie and Uncle Bill, were frugal in every aspect of their being. They were outstanding shoppers, wasted nothing, knew the value of everything, and were savers of the first order. They did not invest in business stocks. Perhaps they had a few shares of the electric company for the dividends. Money in the bank was thought good enough. They had survived the Great Depression and two world wars. They never mentioned these events, but you could see the underlying influences that shaped their thinking.

You did not replace something still workable. You did not buy anything you truly did not need. You paid in cash or you did not purchase. You did not forget those in need. It was amazing to me how little they needed to lead a quality life. Many today would find such a path difficult. However, I have come to realize how personally freeing that way of thinking and lifestyle can be.

A Red-Breasted Robin for Lunch

There were some exceptions to the noon meal regimen. I recall once being at the new Camp with Gordon around noontime. My parents were in Maryland and Gordon had some work to do around the house that would take the whole day. I was free to do as I wished.

Now, my parents would never ever allow me to have a BB gun. Eyes would be put out or brains ruined with these dangerous instruments. No matter how long or how many different ways I tried, that lever action Red Ryder BB gun would never be mine.

This particular year it seems that John and Gordon had discovered they needed to add a BB gun to their arsenal of hunting weapons. I was informed that a BB gun was in fact available for my use. I also recall that this information did not come to my attention until after my parents had gone back to Maryland, leaving me in Kingston under the care and tutelage of John and Gordon.

For the sake of full disclosure, I note, I was not granted access to this BB gun until I had a number of instructional events with real guns provided me over time by Gordon and my father.

This BB gun was not the lever action Red Ryder I coveted. It was a pump BB gun, which was not as cool as the lever action cowboy model, but it worked and it was mine! There are two memorable events concerning this BB gun that I will share, as they reflect on my continuing Kingston education.

On this special day, when I first took possession of my own BB gun, I decided to go on a hunting expedition in and around the Camp property. I remember it was a beautiful, sunny, summer day and I was so glad to be outside at Camp. While in the front yard I noted a huge robin in a tree. Taking quick aim, I fired. The robin dropped to the ground dead. I hit my target on the first shot. I grabbed the still warm robin by the foot and raced inside to show Gordon my trophy. I was so proud.

"Gordon, Gordon, look what I shot!"

Gordon looked over my prey, looked back at me and said: "Good timing. I was just about to fix lunch."

Somewhat bewildered, I followed Gordon into the Camp kitchen. Gordon placed the bird on a wood plank and started pulling out the robin's feathers.

"Are we going to eat the robin for lunch?" I nervously inquired.

"I thought that is why you shot it," said Gordon. "I know you would only shoot what you intended to eat."

I quickly agreed.

Gordon continued to pull the feathers out without looking at me as he spoke. The more feathers he pulled off, the smaller the bird became. When all the feathers were gone, there was almost nothing left. Gordon took out his pocket knife and removed the bird's head and entrails.

"Get me the small frying pan," Gordon instructed.

I did, handing it to Gordon. Gordon poured a touch of olive oil in the pan and turned on the heat. When the pan was hot he put in the robin and let it sizzle and cook. He next removed the bird from the pan, put it on the board, cut the bird in half, and put a half of the robin on each of two plates. We sat with our plates at the kitchen table. Gordon put some salt on his bird and ate it in one bite. I followed his example but had a hard time swallowing. I don't remember if there was any taste to this meal. Lunch was over in less than 15 seconds. We washed off the plates. Gordon resumed his work. I returned to the outside.

I was still hungry. More than that, I was disturbed in a way I did not fully understand. This was not playing cowboys and Indians. I had shot a living, beautiful bird. When I did so, I was not thinking of food. I now felt what I had done was somehow not right. I spent the remainder of the afternoon pondering what happened. After this experience I never shot another bird with a BB gun. I never shot any animal I did not intend to eat. In the end, I learned I did not even like hunting game. I can remember this day as clearly as if it were yesterday.

The BB Gun and the Snake

There was an end to my short lived BB gun adventures. This is a sad but true tale. Just a few days later, after I had recovered from the robin luncheon event, I was roaming outside of Camp. There was a trail from the back property that went to a dirt road that ran behind the Camp. Along this road was an old quarry where bluestone was cut for use in constructing the Ashokan reservoir stone walls. The quarry was now filled with water. I had done a lot of shooting at pretend bad things, totally inanimate objects, on my way to the quarry. I decided I should reload my weapon lest I be caught unprepared and out of ammo. From what evil I was to be prepared for, I didn't know.

To refill this BB gun with the pellets, you had to unscrew a nut on the top of the barrel, remove a spring and a tube, fill it with BBs, and screw them back in the gun. The spring was cocked by the pump action that enabled the gun to fire the BB.

Upon reaching this pond, I started to unscrew the barrel when I thought it best to perform this delicate maneuver while seated comfortably. I was unscrewing the barrel (under pressure from the coiled spring) as I sat down on a rock. The rock moved a little upon contact with my rear end and out from under this rock shot a brightly colored snake. It went between my legs and straight into the water. I jumped in fright just as the spring on the end of the barrel came lose. My fingers came apart. Now I watched as the rapidly uncoiling spring powered itself, the tube, and the locking nut, making a high arch out of the gun barrel and into the air high above my head. My eyes followed the trajectory of parts. The BB gun parts next followed the established laws of gravity. After reaching the full height of the arc powered by the uncoiled spring now spent of its stored energy, these very necessary BB gun parts descended back to earth, landing in the middle of the quarry pond.

This scene played out in my mind several times, but in slow motion. I stood there, mouth open, saying to myself "did this really just happen?" Now, in the middle of this pond, were the snake and the guts to my BB gun. I didn't want the former and could not retrieve the latter. I was in utter disbelief as I assessed the damage to my BB gun. It was now incapable of firing. Where does one buy BB gun parts?

I returned to Camp and confessed to Gordon the story of my adventure. He smiled, grunted, asked no questions, and resumed his work. I still could not believe this degree of misfortune could happen to me. What were the chances of me sitting on this snake's rock at exactly the same time as the barrel and spring came loose? Why did my BB gun parts all have to land in the water and not on nearby rocks where I could easily walk over and pick them up?

I didn't mention to Gordon that we might be able to replace the parts or even buy a new BB gun. Perhaps the Red Ryder model was still possible? No, these thoughts never made it to my lips. I realized I had an opportunity which was now gone. I judged my BB gun activity had concluded all too quickly but I should accept that fate and move on. This ended my experience with a BB gun. I never got the Red Ryder model. It was in fact much easier to load. I did eventually recover from my BB gun melancholia, but it took more than a few days.

An Afternoon Sojourn with Gram and John

As a child I also participated in afternoon trips from the store to Camp with John. Gordon would mind the store for the afternoon and Gram would accompany John and me. She no longer stayed in Camp overnight and was restricted to day visits. She was totally blind and somewhat frail, but with help could make it down the steps to the store and the front sidewalk. Instead of the red J Garbarino & Son pickup truck, we would take the black, four-door 1939 Plymouth sedan with a floor shift. Gram could get in and out of the back seat with assistance and ride comfortably.

Being totally blind, Gram was comfortable moving forward using a shuffle step, which felt safer to her as she could feel her way along the floor with her feet. When moving about the apartment or outside, John would always lead Gram by holding her hands as he walked backwards. When leaving the apartment, we would have Gram back down the narrow stairway. John would go first so he could direct Gram's foot movement, support the bulk of her weight, as we collectively lowered her one step at a time. I would hold Gram's hands so she could pull or push against my strength. Once down all the steps John would take Gram's hands to lead and direct her movement while he walked backwards toward the car.

When returning from an outing, I would hold Gram's hands while backing up the steps. John would be behind Gram, pushing her up one step at a time while she pulled on my hands.

This was the first time I ever had the opportunity to assist the movement of an elderly person. I immediately understood blindness was more than a word. I understood how Gram had to have total confidence in those helping and directing her movement. I also realized how important it was to take Gram on these rides to the Camp and stop for an ice cream. This movement required a lot of effort on Gram's part and she was willing. These trips added both physical and mental stimulation and dimension to her life. I also am convinced it was a key reason why she lived for ninety-seven years.

In helping Gram move as described, I got a chance to hold and study her hands and feel the strength in her fingers. Despite her frailty and age, her hands were strong and her grip firm. It was always clear to me before, but reinforced when I studied her hands, that Gram was a full participant in the operation of the store. These were the hands of a person who worked with them all her life in a greengrocer store. Her hands had character.

Once we were in the car and the drive was in progress, John would provide Gram with a visual description of what he saw and what had changed since their last drive to Camp. He would talk about the stores they passed by on the way out of town and describe who was still in business and how they appeared to be doing. Gram would ask John questions on what he reported. It was clear her memory was not in the least impaired. As we got outside of Kingston, John described to Gram what he observed about the homes of people they knew along the way. John reported to Gram what flowers or trees were in bloom and what had passed.

When we arrived at Camp, John drove the car up the steep driveway of the old Camp and pulled into the small backyard. Gram would be escorted to a seat in the round flower garden between the old and new Camps, on the side opposite the fire pit and the quarry.

John did not come to do maintenance on the Camp as Gordon did. He came to service his flower gardens and plants.

John changed into his work clothes and began to weed, transplant, and trim the flowers and shrubs. As on the ride up, John acted as the eyes for Gram. He described to her each plant, how it looked, what he was doing to it, and how it contributed to the whole of the garden. John also had an assignment for me. I carried buckets of water which I filled from two very large copper rain barrels that collected rainwater from the rear roof of the old Camp. Since it was summer, the plants needed a lot of water when rain was scarce. It was hard work for a young boy to lug all these buckets of water. There was no hose as there was no electric water pump, only the outdoor hand pump. The water from the hand pump was cold, pure and delicious. I later realized that my carrying the water was a real treat for John. If I were not there, he would have to do all the work. I was glad to do it for him. It was not as much fun as hunting with my BB gun, but I learned a lot as he patiently answered my rudimentary questions about flowers and shrubs. To this day I think this experience led to my love of having my own herb and vegetable patch during the summer.

After tending to the gardens and inspecting whatever work Gordon reported to John he was doing at Camp (there was sometimes a discrepancy in what Gordon reported and what was actually done), we put Gram in the car and headed back to Kingston. A few miles down Route 28A, there was a small, one pump gas station that no longer served gas but sold a few sundries along with ice cream. John would pull in and he and I would get ice cream cones for all. This was how I learned John and Gram both had a sweet tooth, with a preference for ice cream. The three of us sat in the car in the dirt parking lot of this small garage and ate our ice cream. Even at this age, I admired John for the amount of work cheerfully done to make Gram's life the best it could be. Whatever John did for Gram, day in and day out, was done with love and patience. John was the principal caregiver for Gram and it was not until I was an adult, with my own aging parents, that I could fully appreciate his willing sacrifice for Gram.

Sometimes at night after supper, John and I would sit outside the store on a bench with the store door open but the lights out. If someone came along needing to make a purchase, John would wend his way through all the produce stored inside for the night to wait on them. Otherwise we just watched the cars (often the same ones) cruising up and down Broadway. I cannot really recall anything of note that we ever discussed, but I do recall these as being very pleasant moments at the end of the day.

If things were quiet John might say "go sit with Gram for a while." I would go upstairs and sit in the rocking chair alongside Gram's bed. "John told me to come up and sit with you." Gram would respond to me in Italian. This is the first person I can ever recall speaking to me in a "foreign" language. I would have to explain to Gram that unlike John and Gordon, I did not understand what she was saying. "Speak English Gram." She would agree to do so. After a few minutes of conversation, or my just sitting there, Gram would say something in Italian and the process would repeat itself.

I was too young to recognize that I could have learned to speak some Italian with Gram's help. I could have enjoyed a more direct relationship with her. I could have asked about her life in Italy and why her parents chose to come to America. Ignorance and lack of direction hindered my opportunity to have Gram's world play an even more important role in my understanding of life in general.

John and Gordon could understand Gram when she spoke in Italian but, as Gordon said, they themselves could speak very little Italian. They grew up in a time when learning the English language was emphasized and had to be mastered by the children in order for them to assimilate and become part of the American fabric. As Gram grew older, and had less interaction with others, she regressed to being more comfortable speaking in her native tongue.

I was well into my career and adulthood before starting my efforts to learn Italian. I continue my efforts today on developing this language skill. I have traveled to Italy over the years and always tried to speak Italian and take advantage of opportunities at the train station, hotel, restaurant or the local coffee shops. Hearing the language all around you helps to develop your ear for learning.

I can state that at all times I have generated a wide range of smiles from the natives who patiently listen to my Italian language efforts. Sometimes the smiles actually turn to laughter, but the Italians love it when you at least try. The worse you speak their language it seems, the more caring and helpful they become.

These efforts brought into focus for me the fact that, despite our language studies in high school or college, most of us in the United States can speak only English. Outside the US, many citizens speak at least two, and more often three or four languages. It is more engaging and fun to try and speak to another in their native language.

1936 photo of the Old Camp, taken from the driveway.

My parents, Joe and DeSales Ring, in front of their honeymoon tent at Camp, July 1937.

Four generations in front of the Old Camp during the summer of 1944. Left to Right: Gram, Aunt Mamie, Elizabeth "Lizzy" Ring (my grandmother), Joseph Henry RIng (my grandfather) and Joe Ring (my father). My brother Dan (left) and I are in front.

Great Uncle Bill rides in the front seat during FDR's election eve visit to Kingston in 1944.

Great Uncle Gordon checking the sights on his bolt action deer hunting rifle.

Great Uncle John holding my brother Dan.

Summer photo at the Old Camp. Great Uncles Gordon (L) and Bill (R) are standing. Seated, left to right, are Assunta "Gram" Garbarino, an unknown lady, and Great Aunt Mamie.

The Old Camp driveway, August 1945, doubled as a social center and was a perfect spot for the author to take batting practice.

Swimming near Great Uncle Bill's Camp at Eddyville on the Rondout Creek, where he created a gravel bottom swim area. My father is at the left with my brother Mike riding the whale. I'm on the right, wearing one of the bulky lifejackets. All you see of my brother Dan are his legs! (1950 photo)

My younger brother Mike (R) and I liked to hang out on the quarry stone wall across from the screened-in front porch.

Gram (L) and Great Aunt Mamie (second from L) pose for a group photo with the ladies of Camp in front of the large gathering tent.

Great Uncle Bill painted this portrait of St. Joseph's Chapel in West Hurley, New York. Uncle John attended this chapel after he retired to Camp.

Sunday Mass at Saint Joseph's

After moving from Selma Avenue to Ellicott City in 1954, my parents, with three boys in tow, regularly attended Sunday Mass at Saint Paul's Catholic Church in Ellicott City. When I was old enough to stay in Kingston by myself, it was understood that I would continue to attend Mass on Sundays. My parents knew that John attended the 7 o'clock Mass every Sunday morning at the St Joseph Catholic Church located in the historic Stockade District of Kingston. It was the oldest part of this early Dutch settlement, located near the Old Dutch Church and colonial burial ground.

So much of my family history was written in St. Joseph's church. The extended Garbarino family was connected to this church and later its grade school, founded just after the Civil War. Here, Garbarino family members were baptized, confirmed, married and eventually prayed for in death. St. Joseph's was to this young boy a beautiful church building surrounded by stately trees and comfortable, well-fashioned homes. The sidewalks were the large, rectangular sheets of bluestone common to the city at that time.

To enter the church you climbed the four or five steps that ran the entire front of the church and entered via one of three large wooden doors. The church years ago added to its original design this front lobby and a bell tower, framed by these three wooden doors.

This first set of wooden entry doors was always open during the summer. Going through these doors, you entered the lobby and found a second, matching set of three wooden doors allowing entry to the church proper. In the middle of this lobby, at seven o'clock on Sunday mornings, stood an eighteen-inch square wooden table, with coins on the top. No sign, no directions, merely coins placed on the table. John would take change from his pocket, put it on the table, and sometimes take change from the table and put it back in his pocket. Then we opened the door on the far right side and entered the church.

I was mystified by this coin table. There was a collection taken during Mass every week and John always put an envelope in the basket. So I deduced the table was not related to the Sunday collection. I had no choice but to finally ask John in the car on the way to Sunday Mass.

"Why do you put money on the table? What are you paying for"? I asked.

"For the seat," John replied.

"You pay to sit in a church to hear Mass?" I asked, never having experienced being charged for a seat in church.

"It's a seat tax. Ten cents apiece. Twenty cents for the two of us."

I had never heard of this before.

"What is a seat tax? We don't have that at home."

John just shrugged. "It is ten cents for each seat and we leave the money on the table. I put in twenty cents for you and me for the seat tax."

"I have never heard of this. We don't have it at our church." I could tell the time for questions with John about this seat tax was over. I would ask Gordon the rest of my questions. He didn't go to church on Sunday, but I thought he probably would know the answers.

Gordon answered my question exactly as John did. I concluded this was a foreign custom not practiced at St. Paul's. As I think about this now, I don't recall ever seeing a seat tax table in any other church I have ever been in.

If the seat tax was a local church custom, John's attendance at the seven o'clock Sunday Mass was in accordance with his personal attendance ritual. It never varied. Upon entering, we made for the last pew on the back right side, just inside the church. To be even clearer, there were no pews behind us and the entire church, usually near empty for the 7 a.m. Mass, was all in front of us. Seated in this last pew were John and I, along with six or seven men all dressed in their Sunday suits, wearing ties and starched shirts, and carrying fedoras. John did a very quick, half genuflection, entered the pew and sat down. I followed. At first, I didn't know any of these men. They looked at me and nodded to John. They knew who I was. No doubt this was the same ritual my father went through at my age. Sometimes a few of the group might occupy the next pew in front of us so there was more room. But no one seemed intent on getting any closer to the priest and the altar.

As a child, under the educational and decorum direction of the nuns, your lips never moved in church unless you were uttering a prayer response. There was no conversation, no giggling, and no form of communication with your fellow classmates. It would, of course, be a boy sitting next to me, as all the girls sat on the opposite side of the church. We had separate gender lines going into, and for seating within, the church.

If anyone uttered anything other than an approved prayer response, the reaction of the overseer nun was often swift, severe and embarrassing. If the violation were severe enough, an ear bash was not unknown. If you did not like the way Sister treated you, appealing to the higher court of parents at home only made the problem worse. Parents always sided with the "mean Sister" and you were often punished twice for the same transgression. Not fair.

With all of this in mind, and being properly habit-formed from youth, I sat quietly next to John. I observed that John must never have been under the direction of nuns. He immediately started gabbing with each and every man in the pew. These men were all older and somewhat hard of hearing. Their "whispers" to each other could be heard clearly echoing throughout the mostly empty church. I always knew John to be a man of few words who never gossiped about another. Now I knew why. He got it all out of his system at the seven o'clock Mass on Sunday mornings with his friends.

When the priest came onto the altar from the sacristy to begin the Mass, the men did stop talking. I now thought they had at least some partial training by the nuns. John had his rosary beads in hand and said the decades during the course of the Mass. The other men sat immobile, at attention, and without displaying any form of reaction to the Mass prayers, the gospel or the ensuing sermon.

The front pews closest to the altar were lightly occupied. The rest of the church was completely empty until our last pews on the back right. Our group would correctly be defined as observers and not overt participants in the Mass. I was always afraid the priest would walk up to me and ask why I was sitting in the back when the whole church in front was empty. What could I say? He or no one else ever asked, so luckily I never had to answer.

In order to satisfy the Sunday Mass obligation, one has to be present for the offertory, the consecration and the communion. You were not required to go to communion, and in fact could not if you were not in a "state of grace." It was easy, I guess, for the busy bodies to speculate about who the sinners were in the congregation. They didn't go to communion. These legal niceties were unknown to me at the time. My experience was you arrived at church before Mass started, and you didn't leave until the priest was off the altar.

At St. Joseph's, as soon as the priest offered communion to the congregation John got up and exited the pew. I immediately followed him, but instead of going toward the altar for communion, John walked through the rear church doors to the lobby, outside, down the steps and into the car. John drove home to fix Gram's breakfast (bacon for all on Sunday, with fresh Italian bread toast).

After experiencing the exact same procedure each Sunday, I wondered why John never went to communion and why he never stayed until the end of Mass. I later found out from Gordon, when I asked about John's church habits, that John was 100 percent legally correct. He did not leave until the communion started. If you were present at Mass for the offertory (collection), the consecration and the communion, you got a check mark for attendance at the compulsory Sunday Mass and avoided mortal sin. As for any further explanation about John's attendance habits, the most I ever got from Gordon was a grunt. If I repeated the question, I didn't even get the grunt. I could think what I wished. There weren't going to be any explanations. Since I knew Gordon did not attend Sunday Mass, I thought it best to learn through observation and not further conversation. I was also beginning to learn that not every one of my questions deserved an answer.

Later, when I had the opportunity to travel through the countryside of Italy and Sicily, I observed that the men who attended the Sunday Mass often congregated at the very rear of the church. Sometimes they actually drifted outside during Mass for a cigarette and a few words with each other, most probably engaging in a commentary on some theological point raised by the Gospel.

I was looking for a Mass one Sunday while in the village of Cefalu, in Northern Sicily. I happened upon a Mass already in progress and again noted the men were standing at the rear of or outside the packed church. There was no entry into the church past these men. As the kiss of peace was being initiated, I was warmly greeted with great affection by what seemed to be every male in the village now present on these church steps. I observed that in general the men here did not appear to sit with the women and children in church. They were very nice people. However, I decided to go to another church whose Mass had not yet started.

Allow me an aside to tell you about my very positive Mass experience in Cefalu. I found the second church (to which I had been initially directed to by the hotel owner) in the heart of the village. I entered to learn from the janitor the next Mass started in one hour. The janitor was busily neatening up the rear of the church and tying the church bell rope to its anchor. I spoke to him in my best Italian and he answered me with a warm smile. You could tell he was a nice man.

Having some time to pass until Mass started, I walked into a coffee shop across the street for an espresso. I stood at the bar while it was being prepared. I noticed the conversation in this Sicilian village coffee shop came to a halt when I entered. Most eyes were upon me. The barman was moving slowly as if trying to decide if he was going to tell me he was out of coffee. I realized I was under suspicion and the men were sorting me out, wondering why I was there. Now, I am an FBI agent working Italian organized crime, and I am in Sicily, the home of the Mafia. But I only want to go to church. Sensing this disquiet on their part, I told the barman in my poor Italian, not in the Sicilian dialect but loud enough for all to hear, that I was a tourist waiting for Mass to start across the street. With that statement all conversation in the coffee shop resumed its previous level of activity, I got my coffee, and the barman went back to his other duties.

I left the coffee shop and re-entered the small church across the street just as a few others drifted in. I sat in a pew, opened a prayer book, and saw the prayers were in Italian. I don't know why I was surprised or what language I expected the prayer book to be in? Next the priest and his server appeared on time from the sanctuary to start the Mass. I realized the person I thought was the church janitor, based solely on his clothing, was in fact the parish priest. It was a poor church.

As the priest approached the altar, he stopped, came to where I was standing, and handed me a prayer book. He turned and went to the altar and began the Mass. I opened the prayer book. This copy was in English. I smiled. I guessed I did not fool the "janitor" with the level of my Italian language capability.

By the end of the Mass it was clear to me this was a wonderful small parish, led by a welcoming priest, and filled with loving members who wanted to be there and participate. They knew there was a stranger in their midst and accepted me from the start. After the Mass ended, I returned the English prayer book to the priest (with some US dollars inserted) and thanked him for his and the church's warm reception. It was a memorable and warm experience where a lack of language ability created no barrier.

Returning to our story, where does this child come out after many years of witnessing one of his favorite great uncles attend Mass in such an unfamiliar manner? The answer was clear. John was one of the most decent, honest, hardworking, quietly generous human beings I had ever met. I watched him night after night with a rosary in his hand, his lips moving rapidly, as he moved through the decades. He gave up his adult life to run the store and assume the responsibility for his mother's care. While he never spent money on himself, he always sent a check to whoever asked. There was no question in my mind, then or now, that John was close to God and a person that I should aspire to emulate in my life.

My Confirmation Name

As mentioned, Gordon did not attend Sunday Mass but I never knew him to do a dishonorable thing. Questionable, edgy, cagey, perhaps less then exactly legal, but not dishonorable. When, at age thirteen, it was time for me to be confirmed by the bishop into the Catholic Church, I chose as my confirmation name Gordon. I explained to our pastor that Gordon was my great uncle who, while not a weekly attendant at Mass, was a good man whom I admired and I wanted to use his name. The pastor said he had never heard anyone using the name Gordon for Confirmation. He needed to check his book of saints to see if the name was appropriate. He returned to the room a few minutes later and said I could use the name. I did. The presiding bishop, when handed the card with my Confirmation name of Gordon on it, did not blink an eye. I was tapped on the cheek by the bishop and my confirmation name was Gordon.

I have been unable to locate a Saint Gordon among the many Catholic saints. I have found no evidence that there ever was a Saint Gordon. Years later I concluded that the good pastor thought it more important that a child take the name of someone familiar and respected to serve as an example.

Gordon the Advisor

I think of my Great Uncles John and Gordon Garbarino as being very much alike in many ways. They shared a common philosophy of life and seemed to have the same relationships with family, friends, customers, and the community in general. In all my years in Kingston I never once heard them argue or offer an ill word toward one another. When they disagreed, it was done quietly and respectfully. If a third party wished to criticize an absent brother in the presence of the other, they had better watch out. A stony silence would indicate the speaker ought to change his topic. Failing that, the speaker would be totally ignored and their presence unwelcome for some time to come.

Who was in charge, you ask? Clearly it was John. He was the second eldest and senior to Gordon by fourteen years. In addition, John was twenty-three when his father died and had worked in the store since graduating high school. Gordon was only nine at the time of his father's death and the youngest child. It was John who took over running the store in 1913, along with Gram, and it was John who committed his life to the operation of the store and to being the primary caretaker of Gram when blindness limited her ability to function. Lizzy was living in Brooklyn, Baltimore, and ultimately Chicago before she returned home to Kingston to die in 1947. Aunt Mamie took a lesser role in the store but lived there, even after marrying Uncle Bill, until they bought 8 Clinton Avenue from the Rings in 1926. After that she was very much a daily visitor to the store.

As a child my memory was that Gordon always lived at the store. I was surprised when I learned there were times when Gordon worked and lived outside the store environment. I recall hearing that for some years he drove a truck. What kind of truck, where, or for whom I have no idea. I asked a few questions but got little more than an acknowledgement from John that Gordon didn't always live at the store. It really was not important to me to know more. He would have been twenty-two in 1926, when Aunt Mamie moved from the store to 8 Clinton Avenue, and Lizzy had moved to Baltimore, leaving John and a healthy Gram at the store.

I mention this history so I can differentiate their leadership roles. John was in charge of all matters relating to store business, finances and the care of Gram. Gordon was in charge of the Camp, vehicles, supplies and non-store administration. Gordon also had a wider range of contacts outside of the store-related community.

As the eldest male, John enjoyed another mantle of leadership recognized by the community. He was able, respected, a sound businessman, a devoted son and regular attendant at Sunday Mass. John was not talkative, but his company was always pleasant and welcome. He was always the more serious of the two brothers, which I think was reflective of the family responsibilities that fell to him. He had a sense of humor that was very dry. Sometimes a few moments would pass before I realized he had just made a humorous comment. Often, I needed to see the smile on his face before I was sure he had just engaged in humor. I never saw him take a drink. He always wore a starched shirt, a clean white apron and a dress felt hat when working in the store. John was a constant in everyone's life.

Gordon was more of a person of the world, so to speak. While he had several long term girlfriends at various points in time, who were well known and liked by the whole family, he chose never to marry. Between the two brothers, Gordon was more of the rascal who felt no need to attend Sunday Mass. He always had time to fish and hunt as he was not as tied to the store, as was John. He went out socially at night with friends during the week and on weekends. He drank, and sometimes too much. Of the two, he was the prankster and the more likely to have a slightly off-color joke to repeat, although such was rare. Gordon had a wide range of knowledge of all things mechanical, electrical and related to construction.

Gordon's opinion was highly valued by those in his circle of friends and acquaintances, the store circle, and among those seeking some type of elusive resource. I would be present when someone would drift by the store about noontime, after Gordon had eaten and while John was upstairs, to have a word with Gordon to elicit some knowledge or advice. I would be with him during the evening when he was with friends and would observe someone having a private conversation with Gordon, seeking his view on some matter. In later years when he hung around the West Hurley firehouse, after the store closed, Gordon was always a person sought out for his opinion. In short, people trusted Gordon, respected his wide range of knowledge and experience, and knew whatever conversation they had with him would remain private. He was not a gossip.

All tribes seem to have a wise, experienced and competent member to whom one can go for advice, without the conversation being made known to the whole tribe. This was one of Gordon's roles. He was Gordon the Advisor.

Later in life, I recognized those same qualities in my own father. At his funeral, I had many people come up to me to tell me stories of how my father had confidentially advised and helped them through some difficult period. In truth, I have seen myself in this role from time to time. I think it was a combination of the dignity of John and the worldliness of Gordon that enabled this advisor role, which was generationally handed down to those in the family who observed and cared.

Let's Go for a Ride

When these words – "let's go for a ride" – were uttered by Gordon after supper, it usually signaled an adventure was at hand. Gordon was always doing things that I had not seen done before, so I was constantly being exposed to new experiences. This was adventure in my book. At this time of the evening, it could mean we were going to visit his girlfriend's house, a friend's bar, or perhaps scout out where the deer were currently feeding and what their exit routes were, as their evening grazing was ending as darkness settled in. It was good to know where the deer were feeding and crossing particular roadways. In military terms, we were gathering intelligence to plot a later strategy for hunting deer.

Now, I will introduce you to the subject of deer hunting as sometimes practiced by the locals, especially during the Depression and other poor economic times when jobs, and sometimes food, were scarce. Some in the crowd of regulars about the Camp were past their prime and found it difficult in their advancing years to take strenuous walks in the woods in search of deer. Many deer hunters find a game trail they know the deer are currently using, hide along that route and wait for a passing deer. The older you get, the more likely you are to place a "stand" or observation and shooting post closer to the road.

Don't forget, the deer you shoot has to be carried or dragged to the vehicle.

If you are participating in a drive for deer using multiple people, the older hunter usually is allowed to wait at the end of the drive area for the deer to emerge after being flushed out. It is this hunter who will have a shot at the exiting deer. This is a form of group hunting where everyone has a role and everyone shares in the bounty.

Gathering intelligence on the current deer population was a year-round affair. The best hunters were able to assimilate data from a wide variety of sources on a continuing basis. This was the Kingston version of real-time data gathering. They knew where the deer were likely to be, or which road they would cross at a given time. Gordon was a recognized expert. He put effort into monitoring the deer traffic patterns all year long. He would share this intelligence with his friends who, if successful, saw that Gordon received some fresh meat.

Sometimes John and I would "go for a ride." His ride was different. We generally saw nothing. When we did see some deer, he would report this information back to Gordon, keeper of all sighting reports. Even with John, knowing we probably would not see any deer, the ride was still an adventure. Being outside in nature as night closed in, seeing the land and the mountains in a different light, all allowed the young mind to create its own adventures. You never knew what may be lurking around the next corner.

One evening at dusk as Gordon and I rode along a dike road on the Ashokan Reservoir, Gordon was trying to look down into a valley of grass below to see if deer were feeding. He couldn't see over the stone wall to the valley below. Both sides of the road were lined with perfectly laid, bluestone walls that so well complemented their natural surroundings.

As noted earlier, the Kingston bluestone quarries and their rail, canal and water access, through Rondout Creek, enabled them to ship bluestone to many eager markets. This included New York City, where many of their early sidewalks were laid with large bluestone slabs cut from Kingston and other nearby quarries.

The car this night was the very same Garbarino-owned 1939 Plymouth, four-door sedan, black, with a floor shift. Gordon had the car in gear and we were creeping along, just above idle speed.

"Here, you steer the car," said Gordon as he opened his car door and stood out on the driver's side running board so he could see over the wall. I was in shock. I had never steered anything before but my bike! Now you want me to steer a moving car! There was no warning, no warm-up period, and no directions. It did not take me long to figure out that my hands on the steering wheel were better than no hands at all. I slid over from the passenger seat and tightly gripped the steering wheel. While I had never heard the term before, this was my first "white-knuckle flight." I was doing great until Gordon said "a little more to the left, closer to the wall."

I thought to myself, "You want me to steer closer to the wall I have been desperately trying to avoid? Are you crazy?"

I said nothing. Breathing was hard enough. I steered us closer to the wall. This dike road was a couple of hundred yards long and we negotiated the entire length with me steering. At the end, Gordon stepped off the running board and back into the driver's seat, relieving me of steering duties. Gordon explained he was able to see the entire area below as we moved along. He said it was better than stopping the car multiple times to look over the wall in different areas. To this day I can't recall what he told me he saw, if anything, in the grass below the wall.

As I grew older I realized how Gordon operated. He would never ask you to do anything he thought you weren't capable of doing. On the other hand, he did not feel it necessary to go into any explanations or provide any advance knowledge or warning of what he would ask you to do. He often had you do little steps that, when completed, signaled to him you were ready for a larger step. Gordon's process was an adventure, but not always fully open to my immediate view. It did create memorable experiences.

These experiences with Gordon impacted things I did with my own children, later with grandchildren, and also with nieces and nephews. When my grandson Liam was a young boy, I had a 14-foot rowboat with a 25-horsepower motor. I made it a point to discuss with Liam boat etiquette, safety, and the purpose of the equipment at hand. One day I said to him while out on the river, "would you like to steer the boat?"

Liam looked at me, digesting what I had asked. He nodded yes. I had him come over and sit with me as I put the motor steering arm in his hand, with mine on top. He felt the way I steered the boat. He felt my hand as I throttled the engine up or down using the same handle. After a few minutes of non-verbal instruction, I took my hand away from the steering arm, saying nothing. I looked about the river while Liam steered. It reminded me of steering the car for Gordon. When we arrived home, Liam mentioned to his mother that he had driven the boat. She looked at me. I smiled. Mom knew it was good stuff. She had seen me in action before.

Introducing a child to an adventure that you know is well planned and safe is one of the great joys of adult life. This I learned not only from John and Gordon, but also from Aunt Mamie and Uncle Bill, as you will later see. I hope they got as much enjoyment from me as I have from my children and grandchildren.

A Man with a Mission to Help

I didn't see Uncle Bill every day. After he ceased being mayor of Kingston, he was active every business day and sat on the board of some local bank. He may even have done some sort of appraisals for them.

One of Uncle Bill's two most important pieces of work at this time in his life was the founding of a group called Gateway Industries. Gateway was devoted to teaching basic living and working skills to those suffering mental disabilities so that they would be able to obtain entry-level manufacturing employment. Their employment, in turn, led them to degrees of personal independence that made their lives more rewarding. They secured training space in Kingston where the attendees reported on a daily basis. Upon completion of a lengthy program, Gateway was successful in placing their students into entry-level manufacturing jobs.

If you wanted to see Uncle Bill's eyes gleam, ask him about Gateway. As a former mayor, he had great contacts in the Kingston area, the Hudson Valley, and across the state. He used them to promote the Gateway program. Uncle Bill was so proud of Gateway and I was so proud of him.

My rides with Uncle Bill often started when he pulled up to the store in his car, parked in front, came in, and greeted everyone. Next, he went to the cigar case, located just to the left of the front door. The cigar case was a small, glass door cabinet located about halfway up the wall, near the area where the paper bags were kept and the customer's order was assembled as they shopped. He would take some cigars, pay John, and ask me, "Want to go for a ride?" Just like when Gordon or John asked the same question, I would always say yes and be eager to be on an adventure with whomever was asking. I looked to John and asked, "Is it okay – do you need me?" John would always answer, "No, I am all set for now." Of course I did not quite realize at this age of ten or so that I was not totally necessary for the successful operation of the store, every moment of the day. Uncle Bill would always tell John where we were going, what we were doing, and when we would be back. "We are going to West Park. I have a meeting, then coming right back."

I later realized that Uncle Bill was recognizing John's custodial role and duties over me and submitted his trip plan for John's approval. Uncle Bill was also showing John respect.

Going to "West Park" meant that we were going to the Sacred Heart Orphanage known to me and most everyone as The Mother Cabrini Home. This was Uncle Bill's second most important piece of public service at the time. The Mother Cabrini Home was located in the hamlet of West Park, in the town of Esopus, on the west side of the Hudson River just north of the Roosevelt family estate, which is on the east side of the Hudson River in Hyde Park.

Uncle Bill always drove a very nice automobile, always in immaculate condition. I clearly remember a Chrysler with leather seats, electric windows, as well as a pushbutton gear selector on the dashboard. These gadgets were all new to me. I was impressed. I asked Uncle Bill many questions while enjoying some of the nicest automobiles in which I have ever ridden.

I can remember our drive along the Hudson River Valley. As I watched him drive I thought to myself, "I see what he is doing. I could even drive this car." I don't have specific memories of the conversations we had on these trips, but I recall the pleasure of touring areas I didn't know and feeling content to be in such warm company.

I also knew as a child that the Garbarino family, because of Uncle Bill, had total devotion to Mother Cabrini. She died in 1917 and in 1946 was the first U.S. citizen to be canonized a saint. It was quite an honor for the Italians to have one of their own, a religious immigrant, recognized for her life's work in helping destitute young women. Any concern a family member needed presented to God was laid in Mother Cabrini's intercessory lap through prayer. Mother Cabrini was a contemporary of Giuseppe and Assunta Garbarino!

Mother Cabrini traveled from Italy to New York City, at the request of Pope Leo XIII, to serve the fast growing Italian population in the New York City area. She brought with her seven Sisters from her order of the Missionary Sisters of The Sacred Heart. They immediately began caring for orphaned or unsupervised young girls in New York City.

By 1890, Mother Cabrini needed more room to care for her young ladies and found this West Park property, which she purchased from the Jesuits who were eager to sell. It seems their well on the property had dried up and they could not locate another suitable well source on the property. Mother Cabrini had faith and bought the land. Since hers was a begging order, it was through begging, augmented by gifts, from which her order obtained the money to buy the property.

Shortly after purchasing the property, a new well source was located! This well source continued to serve their water needs for the duration of the home. I believe Mother Cabrini was most astute when it came to the purchase of property and that God also bestowed great blessings on her efforts to serve these young women from New York City and the area surrounding West Park.

In 1934, a stately brick structure was built. This is the property I remember. It was very impressive to a young boy. I recall it being in perfect condition and clean beyond imagination. The smell inside, of polished wood and wax, permeated. I don't know what Uncle Bill did after we arrived. We would be greeted by a nun, I would be introduced, and Uncle Bill would go off to tend to business while I waited comfortably, often supplied with milk and homemade cookies to help the time pass. I was in grade school at the time, being taught by the Sisters of Notre Dame in Maryland. I "knew" how to behave in their presence and I did here also. I recall the nuns were always very kind to me as I waited. It was also clear they thought a lot of Uncle Bill and treated him with great respect. Since he was not rich, he must have done good work for them.

Everyone in our extended family was provided with multiple forms of Mother Cabrini medals, relics and prayer cards. If there was a problem with any family member in Kingston, or back in Maryland, you can rest assured Mother Cabrini heard about it in short order. Mother Cabrini was highly regarded for the results obtained from the prayers directed to her.

It was not until 1959 that the Mother Cabrini facility and care operation was incorporated as The Saint Cabrini Home. This event brought changes in its governance. The visits I describe took place in the early 1950s. Uncle Bill was one of the many people the Sisters relied upon for help when needed. He served, I believe, on their Board of Directors before and after their reorganization.

Lastly concerning this wonderful institution, I sadly report it closed in 2011.

Uncle Bill and FDR

The date is November 6, 1944. Franklin Delano Roosevelt is running for his fourth and final term as President of the United States. The battle to re-take Europe from Hitler is ongoing and the outcome still not certain. Will the voters want FDR to finish his war effort?

It was an FDR tradition for him to return to Hyde Park on the eve of a presidential election and tour the Hudson Valley prior to election returns being available. This night he spoke at a political rally in Kingston after touring the area in an open car with his host, Kingston Mayor William F. Edelmuth. There is clearly affection between these two political veterans as FDR comments about his congressman (not a political ally) losing his election and the need to build a bridge between Kingston and neighboring Rhinecliff with federal funds after the existing ferry service was eliminated by local government. President Roosevelt went on to praise the work of the marine industry at Rondout Creek and their contributions to the war effort. The crowd is enthusiastic and the turnout strong. No one could guess that in four months this great president would be dead.

I knew Uncle Bill as an ardent supporter of and believer in the politics of FDR, who previously served as the governor of New York. However, Uncle Bill said little within the family about his relationship with FDR. He was not a braggart. I have included in this book a photograph taken the evening of Roosevelt's visit, on November 6, 1944, showing FDR and Uncle Bill touring the Hudson Valley.

The Kingston Daily Freeman noted in its report of the evening activities that FDR was in a "particularly good mood" and appeared in "good health," observations confirmed by the photograph. It is clear that FDR, who seems to have a small camera in his hand, is enjoying a light moment with Uncle Bill, seated directly in front of the president. FDR is portrayed in the news of the day as an "active" campaigner. In fact, both men were quick to smile and enjoy a good political story. In this photograph, you can guess that these men were enjoying a fun moment together during an otherwise difficult time.

Uncle Bill's New York state vehicle license plate was KD-1. Even as a child I knew this was a special license plate. I asked him what his license plate stood for and he said, with a smile of course, "Kingston Democrat number 1." Everybody in the Hudson Valley knew this car.

Learning How to Dress

Uncle Bill was distinguished looking at all times. His remaining hair, of which there was very little, was gray and always neatly trimmed. He was fashionably dressed when tending to his affairs in public during the course of the day. I didn't know what fine wools, soft leather shoes, a fine belt, or well-constructed shirts were at the time. Uncle Bill did not dress like John or Gordon did for work in the store. Even John's Sunday dress clothes for church were not as fashionable as Uncle Bill's. Uncle Bill had a good sense of men's fashion and bought high quality men's clothing.

It took time for me over the years to learn there was good value in buying quality clothing. If properly cared for, these clothes lasted longer, looked better, and contributed to a sophisticated appearance. When Uncle Bill dressed down, as he did when at his Camp on the Rondout Creek, at West Hurley Camp, or in his studio, he always had what I call "a look." Uncle Bill was an interesting and well-rounded person and his clothes contributed to his persona. Now I wonder from whom did Uncle Bill learn his sense of quality and fashion?

Aunt Mamie dressed daily as the senior Italian lady of the family. However, when she went out socially or traveled with Uncle Bill, she wore some very fine suits and dresses complemented by nice jewelry purchased by Uncle Bill over the years. She was short and stout, and, when working at household duties during the day, wore a dress, apron, and thick black shoes with a slightly raised square heel. Aunt Mamie was serious about her duties running her household for Uncle Bill, as well as overseeing John and Gordon's operation above the store. She kept everyone at attention and any lapses of household duties were quickly pointed out.

I remember best the twinkle in Aunt Mamie's eyes. She loved Uncle Bill, and lavished attention on him all the time. At the same time she took great care of John, Gordon and Gram. Aunt Mamie was a worker. She wasted nothing, could shop for a sale with the best, and was gracious and kind to everyone. When Aunt Mamie wanted to say something was expensive, she would use the word "dear." Later, I learned the word "caro" in Italian means dear and, in addition to being a term of affection, is also used to connote expensiveness.

Uncle Bill's Camp

"Want to ride down to Eddyville?" When Uncle Bill asked, I was ready to go. Another adventure! Eddyville was the site of Uncle Bill's and Aunt Mamie's "Camp" on the Rondout Creek, located about ten minutes from their home at 8 Clinton Avenue. Unknown to me at the time, the sanitary condition of the Rondout Creek had deteriorated over the years, caused by industrial abuse and lack of modern sewerage. I always knew my mother was not happy about my going swimming at this Camp and discouraged it without being overtly or loudly opposed in the presence of Aunt Mamie and Uncle Bill. My father appeared neutral to my swimming there, as this was also a place he frequented as a child.

The Camp itself was a small building (shack is more accurate), placed on pilings about five feet above ground. One entered by going up a set of steps and through a small, screened porch that brought you into the living room. Off that room was a tiny bedroom, an even smaller area with a toilet and wash basin, and a galley-size kitchen. There was electricity but oil lanterns were often in use. That was it. It was a tiny cabin.

Just before going down the gravel lane that led from the road to the Camp, Uncle Bill stopped the car at the side of the road where a pipe came out of a very high rock wall. This pipe flowed with fresh spring water. The water from the Rondout Creek was not potable so Uncle Bill carried water containers in the trunk, which we filled and carried into the Camp to use for our drinking water. I had never seen a spring like this before. The pipe came out of rock and was constantly flowing with sweet drinking water. I never had to gather my drinking water from a spring before. Gathering water like this was part of the adventure. River water was pumped in and used to flush the toilet.

I remember that as soon as we arrived, Uncle Bill changed into his nautical style work clothes. Dungaree pants and shirt, a nautical cap, and slip-on leather boat shoes. There was always something to repair or some improvement being worked on.

Uncle Bill had both a fixed and floating dock. As I noted, the cabin was on pilings. Uncle Bill's fixed dock was high enough to avoid damage during flood stages of the river. The Hudson, into which the Rondout empties, is tidal and thus the tide enters the Rondout. During storms, the river has been known to flood and Uncle Bill avoided flooding problems by being high enough off the ground with the Camp, the fixed dock, and also by having a floating swimming dock that allowed for high tide or flood upward movement.

As a child I was much impressed by these docks. It is where people spent most of the time in good weather. The fixed dock had some built in seating and some chairs. There was an outdoor fire pit in the yard between the cabin and the fixed docks used for cookouts.

Uncle Bill had two boats docked at his Camp at various times. One was a wooden inboard motor boat, about 16-feet long. It was beautiful with fine, polished wood siding, a covered bow, and front and back row seats. It had a steering wheel and chrome bow lights that were as sleek as the boat itself. I have seen other lake boats of this same style over the years and they are now very collectable and expensive.

Uncle Bill also had a 28-foot cabin cruiser periodically docked at Eddyville. It was owned by him and a friend of his who owned a business in Rondout. Uncle Bill would often just tinker with or clean his boats, and I was most happy to be his assistant. I can remember going out on the smaller boat a few times but never on the cabin cruiser. Once a year Uncle Bill and Aunt Mamie would join other boats on the river for a group trip down the Rondout Creek to the Hudson River, and then head north up the Hudson, using various routes, to the Great Lakes.

Uncle Bill had served in the Navy during World War I. I believe he was aboard the USS Adams, which was used as a naval training ship berthed in New York Harbor during the war. He was very active with local and statewide veterans groups for the rest of this life. Uncle Bill did enjoy his Camp at Eddyville, his boats, and knew enough to be able to navigate these boat trips up the Hudson River.

My mother made me promise that if I "had" to go swimming at Eddyville, I would wear a life jacket. "But Mom, I can swim." It did no good: no life jacket, no swim. That was the rule and Uncle Bill and Aunt Mamie would enforce it. Uncle Bill had some huge World War II surplus life jackets worn by US military. They were not child size and I always felt like I was swimming with a floating bear around my neck and back. However, they did work well. Sometimes Uncle Bill would leave Aunt Mamie and me there alone while he had to go out. I would get bored and pester her to go swimming off the dock. Eventually she would give in. I would put on the life jacket, submit to inspection, and down the floating gangplank we would walk.

Just imagine, Aunt Mamie is in her work dress and apron, wearing her stout, square-heeled black Italian shoes, and trying to walk down a floating dock. She would watch as I jumped off the front of the dock, swam around and came out on the side of the dock where there was a ladder to climb out of the water. I would do the same thing five times or so before Aunt Mamie would ask if I was finished. I did not want to hurt her feelings by telling her I could do this all afternoon.

"Do two more and we'll go back and dry off," Aunt Mamie would say.

"Yes, Aunt Mamie," I would reply, without argument.

I knew she was not comfortable with me jumping into the water, even with a life jacket on, but I knew also she wanted me to have a good time. I could tell my swimming made her nervous. Years later, it occurred to me Aunt Mamie may not have known how to swim or was just not physically capable of doing so at this stage in life. In any event, I always loved her for not saying no to me.

I think of Aunt Mamie and how I am sure allowing me to swim off the dock with no one else around was an effort for her. This is another act of kindness and love by a great aunt remembered many years later.

The Adventure of the Mean Nurse

When I was eleven or so, I arrived at Kingston earlier than usual that summer. I knew in advance my parents were dropping me off and would not return until weeks later for their vacation and to pick me up. I was in heaven thinking of the time I would get to spend with everyone at the store, Camp and Eddyville. I knew I would be the focus of their attention and that was fine by me. What adventures lay ahead!

I was surprised to find a bicycle propped up against the tree outside the store. No one said anything about it and I didn't ask. At the end of the day it was placed inside the store. I decided now to ask John about the bike.

"Whose bike is that? What's it for?"

"You ride a bike, so in case we need to have errands done you can use the bike."

"You mean it's for me to use?"

"Yes."

I was striking it rich. This was going to be a great summer. I now had pedal power in Kingston and did not have to walk everyplace.

There was a trap door in the store floor behind the front window. Over the years I had seen John lift it up and go down into a cellar but had never been down there myself. Finding myself alone in the store

119

one day after "chasing the broom" (John's instruction to me to sweep the store floor), I decided to check out what appeared to be an interesting cellar. I opened the door, walked down the steps, and found somewhat of a dirt floor cellar with some miscellaneous items that appeared to be for winter use in the store. There was also a barrel lying on its side in a cradle with a spigot on its front face. There was a cup on the shelf below. Something to drink stashed here in the cellar I thought. Probably water but maybe moonshine? Why I had the last thought I will never know. I put some in the cup, took a sip, and immediately realized how stupid I was. It was kerosene used for winter lamps and heaters.

As I spit out this vile tasting liquid I realized how lucky I was that it was only kerosene. How dumb was I to drink an unknown liquid. I knew this action would not make John and Gordon think I was grown up enough for the affairs of the store. I concluded they should never know. I said nothing to them of this adventure, or misadventure, as you might more appropriately call it.

The kerosene experience came to mind a day or so after my arrival this particular summer when I saw John open the trap door and go down the stairs into the cellar. I edged over to the side to see what he was doing. He had his face in his hands, standing in the middle of this small area, and was crying. I eased back from my vantage point feeling that I had seen something not intended for me to see. What to do? I had no one to ask. A short while later John ascended the steps into the store and closed the door. He knew I could see he had been crying. I felt so badly for him. I had to see if I could help him?

"John, what is wrong? Can I help?"

John waited a few seconds before responding. I could tell he was thinking.

"Gordon has bleeding ulcers and has to be operated on. If he doesn't have the operation he can die. He can also die from the operation. It's serious and I am scared for him."

I realized I was now having a very real adult conversation and was not sure I was prepared for it. What was the protocol? What was proper for me to say? My doubts about what to say or do lasted about five seconds. I just started being myself.

"How can I help Gordon?"

"He will be operated on in two days. I cannot leave the store and Gram to be there. Can you go to the hospital and call me to let me know how he is? Aunt Mamie will be there also but I want to hear what you see and hear."

"Sure, where is the hospital and how do I get there?"

'It's the Kingston City Hospital, up past the theater on Broadway."

"Sure, I can walk that (about a ten minute drive but a 45 minute walk).

"You don't have to walk. I bought the bike so you could ride it up to check on him."

It slowly dawned on me that I was there for an extended summer stay for a reason. My parents must have known about Gordon's operation when they brought me to Kingston but were going to let John explain the situation to me. Gordon was very sick and John could use a runner, an errand person, a helper. I was glad to have been chosen for the assignment.

"Whenever you want me to check on Gordon let me know. I'll hop the bike and ride up there. Anything I can do John, just let me know."

That seemed to be a natural end for this conversation and we returned to store business without further discussion. When I saw Gordon next, I told him that I would be coming to the hospital to check on him so I could report back to John. He smiled, nodded, and that was the end of our conversation about any upcoming operation.

I had no idea what a bleeding ulcer was. But I knew it was not good.

The day of Gordon's operation came. John was edgy and nervous. It was to be a lengthy operation and Mamie would call as soon as it was finished. She did telephone as promised and talked to

John. He did not seem relieved but just told me it was over and Gordon was in his room (translated, he is still alive).

A short while later John said "why don't you take a ride up?"

"Sure, John."

It was mid-afternoon. I peddled to the downtown area of Kingston toward the Rondout section. I had never done this before and was not sure of where I needed to go or exactly what I was supposed to do. In short, I had no detailed instructions. But I was on a mission for Uncle John and was not to be deterred by ignorance, lack of knowledge or effort!

There was an information desk in the hospital main entrance lobby, which I approached.

"I need to find out about Uncle Gordon. Uncle John sent me. He had an operation today."

The lady smiled. I was all business. "What is his last name?" (I forgot not everyone in Kingston would know my uncles).

"Gordon Garbarino."

She gave me his room number but told me visiting hours for the afternoon would end shortly.

"I am not visiting. I just want to know how he is so I can tell John." I could not understand why she wanted to complicate my mission.

I was in a hallway where there seemed to be a lot of sick people. I found his room. He was lying in bed asleep, hooked up to tubes and machines. As I stood in the doorway just staring, a nurse came by and asked what I wanted. I explained my mission. She told me the former mayor's wife, Mrs. Edelmuth, had just left.

"What do I tell John?"

"So far so good. We will know more in the next day or so."

She was a nice lady. I had a report for John from an official person. On the bike, I pedaled as quickly as I could back to John. He was anxious to hear what I had to say and seemed a little happier after my report. He had talked to Mamie who apparently told him the same thing. I think John knew Aunt Mamie might fudge her answers a little so John would not worry so much. He knew at this point in my life deception was not yet a developed behavior.

That same evening John said, "Why don't you take another ride?"

"Okay." I was on the bike and away. It was still light out; the summer was just starting.

There was no one at the desk in the hospital lobby. There seemed to be no one around. I had the room number memorized so I proceeded directly there. I noticed a few of the staff looking at me as I was trying to find Gordon's room. I found him. He looked the same. A nurse came by, so I was happy that I would get another report for John.

"You aren't supposed to be here. Who are you?" she snarled.

I gave her my name, and told her I was checking on Uncle Gordon so I could report back to Uncle John.

"You have to leave. Visiting hours are over. You can't be here."

"I'm not visiting. I am checking on Gordon. He is still asleep and can't visit with anyone."

She was a mean person. I did not like her. I was taught to respect my elders but she seemed to enjoy being mean.

"Leave."

"What do I tell John?"

She harrumphed away, went to a desk and told another nurse, "Get that kid out of here."

That nurse got up from her desk and came to where I was standing. I explained to her why I was there. She said Gordon was okay but that I needed to leave. She told me the visiting hours. I told her I was not visiting and left.

Evening was fast approaching as I pedaled back to the store. There were plenty of street and store lights on so I could see without a problem. It was fun and different for me to be riding a bike at night. I got back to the store and told John what the second nurse had to say. I didn't mention the mean nurse. I did not want to worry him.

The next afternoon John asked me to ride up to the hospital and get a report. Aunt Mamie had been there earlier but was now home. I knew it was now between morning and afternoon visiting hours and that was why Aunt Mamie had left. Rather than tell John about visiting hours, I just left.

When I walked into the hospital lobby, I tried to look like I knew exactly what I was doing. I walked with purpose toward Gordon's room. As I walked past the nurses' desk, down the hall from Gordon's room, I did so with all the authority an eleven-year-old could muster. Gordon was awake, sort of.

Gordon smiled when I walked in.

"John sent me to find out how you are doing."

Weakly, he responded he was doing "fine." "Tell John I am getting better."

"I will." I got my report so I thought I should get while the getting was good.

I made another trip that afternoon, during visiting hours, so I had nothing to worry about.

That evening John asked me to go back for the third time that day. I knew the mean nurse would be there. Oh well, I would just deal with it. Away I pedaled.

Walking down the hospital hallway towards Gordon's room, I noted the mean nurse was not with the others. One smiled at me and the other put her head down so she would not see me. I had some allies!

Into Gordon's room I went. He was pretty much awake and, while still sick looking, he looked more like himself than he had earlier. Gordon told me to tell John he was much improved. I knew that wasn't exactly true but I would carry the message as dictated.

Gordon was asking about Gram and the store when the mean nurse walked in.

"I told you last night you cannot be here after visiting hours," she said.

"I am not visiting. Uncle John sent me to find out how Uncle Gordon is doing."

I could tell this nurse was used to getting her own way. She started yelling at me, telling me unaccompanied kids were not even allowed. I had no right. She would tell my parents.

"They are in Baltimore now but will be back in about six weeks," I replied.

I was beginning to realize I could get under her skin and now that is exactly what I was going to do.

As she continued to yell, I calmly ignored her, turned to Gordon, and asked him if there was anything else I should tell John for him. He was now grinning but I could tell even doing that was causing him pain in his stomach.

I turned and left. The nurse stood in the doorway continuing her yelling. As I walked past the nurses' station on the way out, they did not look up. They kept their heads down but were quietly laughing. I had allies in this battle.

John was so happy to hear my report, without of course, any reference to the mean nurse. He sent me up the street on my bike to the ice cream store to bring back a quart of vanilla. John, Gram and I were going to celebrate the good news with some ice cream. We had no freezer at the store so that meant we had to finish off the whole quart. The three of us did. No problem. After the extended bike riding and nurse confrontations, this ice cream tasted extra special.

By now I was making three trips a day to the hospital. Gordon was starting to get better. John told me I didn't have to talk the whole time; I could just sit there and keep Gordon company. This was similar to what I did with Gram, from time to time. I found that keeping someone who is sick company is a wonderful thing to do. It also makes you feel good.

It was the last trip of the day John wanted me to make that always put me in conflict with the mean nurse. When I walked in again that night after visiting hours, the nurses at the station pretended I did not exist. I sat in Gordon's private room and we quietly talked. I told him about everyone who came into the store, who was asking for him and sent their regards. He gave me messages to take back.

The mean nurse walked in, glared at me, and started to turn ugly. I would not even look at her. She started to say something but Gordon caught her attention and just looked at her. The nurse growled, turned on her heel, and left. That was the last interaction I ever had with this nurse. She did see me there more nights, as Gordon was in the hospital for an extended period. However, she always looked down or in another direction.

It was not until Gordon was home and really on the road to recovery that he told John the stories about my difficulties with the mean nurse. Later, I got the drift that Uncle Bill may have contacted the director of Kingston City Hospital to discuss the behavior of this officious City of Kingston nurse, and her attempts to thwart my efforts to obtain status reports for John. Whatever happened, she was no longer interested in interfering with my regular visits to Gordon's hospital room.

Going Back Can be Difficult

One of the pictures I have included was taken of me and my two brothers "swimming" in the Rondout Creek while being supervised by our father. To the immediate left of Uncle Bill's cabin in Eddyville was a gravel area he put in for wading and to launch boats. It covered an otherwise muddy river bottom

Fifty-eight years later, I tried to locate and visit Uncle Bill's Camp in Eddyville. I started from the house at 8 Clinton Avenue and made turns in the car as the recall of my childhood memory allowed. I remembered the winding road that took us into the Rondout area. I knew which way to turn when I reached the Rondout Creek. I was shocked when I observed all the abandoned docks, cranes, half-sunken barges, and rusting industrial waste all now at the water's edge. This was the industrial area of the Rondout section that was no longer suited for today's river commerce. Closer to where the Rondout Creek met the Hudson, certain areas were being rehabbed into a more fashionable art colony incorporating a village lifestyle.

As we proceeded along this road, I could not get my bearings. My instinct was running low. I think I was distracted by the gruesome scene of industrial waste before me. Eventually, I crossed a bridge over the Rondout and a small waterfall. I immediately knew I had gone too far. That waterfall was just above Uncle Bill's cabin. I remembered stories of years gone by where small boats came to these falls to fish shad in order to get their roe. I needed to turn around and go back, which I did. I next recalled the solid rock wall with a spring water pipe sticking out, which was located just where I should turn into a gravel driveway. I started looking for the pipe. Good move. I found it!

At that point I knew the driveway to Uncle Bill's cabin was just across the road. At the end of a gravel driveway I saw camper vehicles spread along the river bank. The area was now a campground. There were motorboats docked at individual slips all along the property's edge. I got out and walked around. I was trying to get my bearings so I looked for the building showing partially in the back of the photograph, which was just across the small bay behind where Uncle Bill's cabin should be. I looked. There it was. I knew I was standing almost where the cabin should be, but it was not there. What I did see was the crushed gravel bottom wading area and boat ramp depicted in this photo. I had my bearings at last. I next saw a huge weeping willow tree, which I recalled from my childhood memory was located between the cabin and the fixed portion of the dock. Where was the dock? Next I began to see a row of pilings sticking out of the water. Their line was still straight but their tops had worn away over the years. I knew I was now standing on the spot where the cabin should be. I saw a man lounging nearby. He appeared to be a campground regular, well ensconced in his little space.

"Been coming here long?" I asked.

"Oh, yea. Long time. Nice spot," was the reply.

"Wasn't there a cabin right over there?" I said, pointing next to the ramp area.

"Oh, yeah. There was an old shack over there used by the campground owners for storage. They tore it down last year. It was falling apart."

I started to tell this person it was not a shack! It was a cabin with a great history and plenty of wonderful family memories. Somehow

I didn't think he would be interested so I said nothing. I could now clearly see the entire outline of Uncle Bill's Camp. This was my first time back in probably forty years.

This section of the river was now fairly clean. The river came over the small falls, past Uncle Bill's, down toward the old industrial area, past Rondout and out to the Hudson. It was a nice campground. I felt like getting up on a tree stump and telling those present they were on hallowed ground, a valuable piece of property. Instead I just absorbed my surroundings, felt both joyful and sad memories, got in the car and drove away.

As I was leaving I thought of the time my father and Uncle Bill went off in the smaller boat to get a "flagpole." They said they would be back in a short time and that I could play in the area until they returned, but to stay out of the water. No problem.

Instead they were gone a long time and I was getting hungry. There was a pack of hot dogs on the counter they were going to cook up for lunch. I didn't think it would be a good idea to use the gas stove, so I decided to see what a raw hot dog would taste like. When you are really hungry they are not bad, especially if you put a little mustard on them. After a few hot dogs eaten this way, I didn't feel that well.

I heard their boat returning and went out to the dock. Dad had a long pole secured by rope to a stern boat cleat so they could drag the floating pole behind the boat. As the story unfolded during their unloading and placing of the "flagpole" on the dock, I learned that Uncle Bill had spotted a mast on a mostly-sunken old, wooden sailboat down the river. Since it was not doing anything useful, Uncle Bill thought it would make an excellent flagpole for the fixed portion of his docks. Indeed it did, and remained standing there for many years. But now it was gone. Perhaps, I thought hopefully, someone else is using it today as their flagpole.

The Garbarinos and the Game Wardens

While deer hunting was a much discussed subject at the West Hurley Camp, so was the subject of fishing. Because the Ashokan Reservoir is a vital New York City water supply, the regulations about its role in nature and for local community use were somewhat strict. Hours of permitted fishing did not include the hours just before sunup or just after sundown. These are of course prime times to go fishing! Uncle Gordon told me how he and Uncle Bill would get dropped off by the dam, separating the upper from the lower basins, so they could fly fish at night.

I enjoyed Gordon's stories about ducking the game wardens that were looking for miscreants, just like him and Uncle Bill. I asked directly, as a child might, if they had ever gotten caught. I received less than a direct answer and now as I reflect, years later, I think sometimes the game warden won.

As noted earlier, current deer feeding habits were a much discussed subject at Camp. As the weather turned cold and winter set in, prior noted and recorded deer habits formed the basis for current hunting plans. There are various ways to hunt deer. Some hunters go solo and will mount a stand in a tree overlooking active deer trails.

They remain in the stand until a qualified deer wanders by and they shoot it with a scoped high power rifle. It doesn't seem to me like a lot of skill is involved. Of course the deer then has to be dragged back to wherever the transportation is located, which is often physically difficult even after the deer has been field dressed.

Some hunters may band together and perform a drive. Hunters basically form a line and march through a defined area, hoping to scare the deer, or even a herd of deer, into moving toward the shooters' position, well ahead of the drivers. As a child I participated as a driver (sans gun) with young legs. Once we jumped several deer and when they took off they went to our left rather than straight ahead toward Gordon, who was the designated shooter. It seems the man shoring up the left flank had failed to keep up with the line and all the deer ran out of the drive area through his position. An error such as this is cause for much grumbling and muttering later at night.

For me, to go deer hunting in Kingston was a treat as normally I was at home in school at this time. There were a few winters where Dad wanted to go to the Camp and hunt, and a trip would be set up over school vacation so the family could go. Most of those who visited John and Gordon's Camp were very cautious about hunting during the official weeks of deer season, especially if it required going into the woods. Being 91 miles from New York City, we were just close enough to the Big Apple to suffer all the yahoos looking to shoot their first buck. Often regaled with the finest in hunting attire, and carrying the most powerful weapons, these hunters often knew little of the area they were in, much less how to safely hunt that area. They were considered a clear and present danger.

During this period, it was not unknown for locals to keep an unloaded rifle on the front seat with a loaded clip in a shirt or jacket pocket. Should one happen upon a grazing deer not far off the road, the rifle could be loaded, fired, the deer dropped and dragged to the vehicle, in a very short period of time. Smaller caliber weapons were popular as they made far less noise. The target for this type of weapon was the deer's head. Hit it and the small caliber rifle was effective. Miss and the deer got to walk away until the next time. It was a one-shot deal.

The Deer Who Walked Away and My First Shot of Whisky

Having described above some methods used to hunt deer, I may as well confess the story of the day I took my first shot at a live deer. It was also the day I had my first drink of whisky.

I was fourteen and my brother Dan was sixteen. We were at Camp with our father, Gordon, and long-time family friend Larry Machione. It was hunting season and it was decided we would go out hunting early in the morning in two cars. Larry and I would go in one and Gordon would drive Dan and my father. We would not be going into the woods. There were a number of gravel-dirt roads that wove around the Camp area that were perfect for hunting deer, shall we say, somewhat by car.

It was a cold morning as we rode along with the windows down and the car's heater on full blast. Larry drove (I was too young) and there was an empty 30.06 sitting between us. Larry had a loaded clip in his pocket. As we drove the cold dirt-gravel crunched under our tires as we slowly moved along, each one taking a side of the road to search for deer. The immediate edge of the road was bordered closely with light forest and heavy brush.

Larry slowed the car. We both saw a young buck about fifteen yards into the brush on my side of the car. He was just looking at us as we looked at him. Larry handed me the clip and slid the rifle off the seat into my hands. I quietly slid the clip into the rifle. As I raised the rifle to look through the scope, I realized I was not going to be able to fire from my right shoulder as I could not turn that much in the car to square up to the deer, which remained motionless.

I mounted the rifle to my left shoulder, looked through the scope, and found that the deer was still just looking at me. I put the crosshairs on the deer's head, kicked off the safety, and pulled the trigger.

CLICK! The sound of a firing pin falling on an empty chamber is much louder than you might think. It has an embarrassing loudness to it. I knew right away I had inserted the clip but not chambered a round into firing position. I looked at Larry.

"Try using a bullet. The deer is still there," he said.

I chambered a round using the bolt action. It made a solid gun noise. The deer remained in the same motionless position. I mounted the rifle to my left shoulder for the second time, found the motionless deer in the scope again. It had not moved and was the same fifteen yards away. I put the scope crosshairs in the center of the deer's head, kicked the safety off again, and fired.

The report from the gun fired from inside the car was very loud. The recoil raised the scope from my eye so I could not see the deer in the scope. I lowered the rifle to see where it fell. The deer was still standing there motionless, just looking at us. It next turned its head slowly and walked off into the deeper brush and out of sight. It didn't run, it didn't even saunter; it walked away!

I made no effort to chamber another round. It was either a head shot that dropped the deer in its tracks or the deer got away. One shot. My first shot at a deer with a scoped rifle fifteen yards away and I missed. I was in shock.

I opened the bolt, dropped the clip, and handed it back to Larry. "How did that happen, I asked?"

Larry was kind. "There was more brush than you thought. When you looked through the scope you could not see all the brush but you could see the deer clearly. I think your bullet was deflected by the brush. It does not take much to change the bullet's flight path."

Was it possible? Was this just a face saving excuse? I knew I was going to be the subject of some humor. That was okay. I could take it.

Not far from where we were was Dr. Kelly's house. Dr. Kelly worked in New York City and was frequently at his beautiful, native-stone country house on weekends with his wife. He was well liked in the community and had been a fixture for years. As we edged by, we noticed Gordon approaching from the other end of the road. Dr. Kelly was on his front porch, waving us in.

"How about a hot coffee?"

By now it was probably seven-thirty in the morning. It was cold. We all piled into the kitchen. Dr. Kelly put the coffee pot on the counter with some cups for all to pour. He stepped into the next room and returned a few moments later with some shot glasses and a bottle of whisky.

"A little something for the cold out there?"

Dr. Kelly placed a shot glass in front of each person, including Danny and me. We remained silent as he filled each glass. Neither Gordon nor my father appeared ready to offer any instruction to Danny and me. The coffee tasted strong, even with a little sugar added. The whisky went down in one gulp after everyone toasted to the hunt. My first whisky! Could not have been a better experience.

Dr. Kelly spoke. "I thought I heard a shot out there?"

The room remained quiet. It was my story to tell so I best get on with it.

I told everyone what happened without emotion, complaint or question. "And after I finally got the shot off, the deer was still just standing there!" I said shaking my head.

Larry spoke next. "There was a lot of brush. The shot was good, it was the brush."

A little more coffee and we were back on the road. There was no further talk of the missed shot, just the expectation of where the next one might take place.

My Last Shot at a Live Deer

If you the reader are curious and would like to know the story about the last time I shot at a live deer, please read the above story again! The above described shot was not only my first but also my last effort ever to personally shoot a deer.

I would not like to leave the impression that Camp and Kingston passed on to me a love of hunting. I soon realized what I enjoyed about hunting was being outside with nature in the peaceful woods. I could enjoy that without a gun. I did not need to hunt to put meat on the table. I could be in the woods anytime I wished. Enjoying nature outdoors, not hunting, is what Camp embedded into my DNA.

I will admit that I do like to fish. I started out in freshwater trout streams and more recently have turned my hand and rod to saltwater fly fishing. I took my son and daughter trout fishing when they were very young. My son Brian takes my two granddaughters, Grace and Anne Marie, fishing to this day. The gene was passed on. However, I don't get to fish a lot and even when I do I don't often have to worry about cleaning caught fish. I think my fondness for fishing is more about enjoying the outdoors.

The Resurrection

My younger brother Michael has one of the best Camp deer hunting stories of all times. It started as usual with Gordon saying to him one hunting season, "Let's go for a ride?" Michael was all in.

I will note at this point Gordon is no longer physically capable of walking very far in the woods or dragging a deer anyplace, much less out of the woods. A young, strong man like Michael was just what Gordon needed to share the hunting duties.

Gordon and Michael have the store truck and a rifle firing .22 longs on the seat between them. Gordon has a clip in his shirt pocket. According to Michael, it was a picture perfect set up. On the dirt road behind Camp up toward the gorge, Gordon spots a deer about twenty yards off the road. Gordon moves like a snake, has the gun loaded, a round chambered, safety off, and the scope crosshairs on the deer's head. Zing. The shot is off, the deer drops; Michael lugs the now dead deer the short distance back to the truck. Michael throws a tarp over the deer to avoid any nosey inquiries. Gordon says they will drive to the Camp and gut it there. Gordon drives over the gorge bridge and heads back to Camp via the spillway road.

Michael is riding on the back of the truck as we always did. Everyone could tell when we were visiting. They would see us on the back of the truck.

As they ride along Michael notices the local game warden, in his marked vehicle, is now driving in the same direction and just behind the truck. The deer is "legal" since it was shot by a hunter with a license and in season. Exactly from where or how the deer was shot leaves open some questions of hunting law. Gordon never drives fast. Michael is feeling a little guilty just because he is under direct observation by a game warden and traveling with Gordon, who enjoys a certain reputation as a rascal of sorts. Michael looked from side to side trying to find something on the roadside to admire so he is not in the game warden's line of sight. Next Michael feels a stirring at his feet. The dead deer under the tarp starts moving. Michael concludes the deer is no longer dead but alive. He discreetly passes this information on to Gordon, who merely nods. There is nothing either can do. Michael tries to give the deer a kick without the game warden noticing the continued deer stirrings. This is not going so well. There is nothing Gordon can do but follow the World War II advice of Winston Churchill to the English people during the German V-2 rocket blitz of London: "Stay Calm; Carry On."

Michael continues to keep both feet on the deer to prevent it from moving. Gordon slows down a little to see if the game warden wants to pass him. He does not. Gordon putts along doing nothing more until they come upon the driveway to the old Camp. At the time there was a sharp climb from the road to the top of the driveway, which when reached puts the vehicle out of view of the road traffic.

Gordon made the right hand turn up the driveway. The game warden did not. The deer was forthwith dispatched to insure there was no future resurrection of this animal. It was temporarily hung up in the garage with the blackened windows. They would return shortly to gut and clean the deer and then hang it outside to cure the meat for a short while. After all, it is hunting season and the deer is legal?

Two Defining Events

After Gram died in 1959, the store was demolished within a year and John and Gordon "retired" to the Camp. These two events changed all that Kingston meant to four generations. They are two defining events.

We were all grateful that our blind Gram died just before she would have witnessed her tiny apartment over the little greengrocer's store, her home for almost sixty years, reduced to rubble and flattened, in a matter of minutes, by a backhoe. It would have been very difficult for her to acclimate to life in the new Camp, which was not even there when she was sighted.

I was sixteen years old when Gram died. I have no memory of our trip to Kingston for her funeral. I have no memory of who came to the funeral home the night before the burial, or even where we stayed. Did we all stay at Camp? Was there room? I know the funeral Mass was attended by a number of area priests and politicians but I have no specific memory of her funeral Mass at St. Joseph's. I have no memory of the procession to St. Mary's Cemetery. None of these things, which I know all happened, are present in my memory bank.

What is present in memory bank? I have only one memory of Gram's funeral. I vividly recall a scene, which is still firmly etched into my mind and could have taken place yesterday. John and Gordon were walking back from Gram's grave site after the internment to a waiting, large, black limousine. John and Gordon are holding each other, supporting each other, arm in arm, and both are openly weeping. They are stooped over, barely able to walk except for each other's help. They are not the strong virile men of my childhood memory. They are shattered remnants of what I knew. John and Gordon are two aging men who lived alone with their mother, never married, saw to her care, and now their entire lives were in the throes of great change at an age when change will be challenging. Gram was gone. The store was near its end. They would "retire," whatever that meant. They didn't know. They would just go to Camp and live on one day at a time. They never really had a retirement plan for "after the store."

I was a junior in high school and knew I had to return immediately to school from the funeral. I never said "goodbye" to my much loved Joseph Garbarino greengrocer store at 784 Broadway. When I learned it was to be torn down after Gram died, I did not go back for a last look, a final visit. After Gram's funeral, and the sight of John and Gordon struggling back to the limousine, I wanted to remember the store, the times there with Gram, John and Gordon, as they were in my mind. I wanted to remember the store as active, alive, exciting, and the source of new experiences. I did not want to disturb these memories with someone's need to build yet another traffic intersection in a futile effort to prop up yet another decaying American town. I chose not to say goodbye. I wanted no final viewing of the store. I am not sure today it was the best way to handle the demise of 784 Broadway, but it was the only way I could at the time.

If someone had asked me at the time how these two defining events impacted me, I would have said I was sad. However, I now more accurately realized, after seeing John and Gordon in these circumstances, my heroes, I was greatly depressed.

I was no longer a child and had to start making a serious effort to adjust my mindset to a new realty. I could not bring back the past and needed to be thankful for what was left of this wonderful childhood experience.

Memorial Day Flowers

John and Gordon continued some of their store-related commercial ventures into retirement. For as long as I could remember, they had clients for whom they would fill family cemetery urns with flowers and neaten the gravesites of departed family members. This was a point in time when people still visited the gravesites of family members. Memorial Day was a time to remember deceased family members and those who had fallen in military service to our country. Today it is the military veterans who keep Memorial Day alive in this country. We owe them a great deal.

Gordon particularly liked to refurbish cemetery urns for their clients. Families were busy enough with daily life, which required them to hire someone to perform this chore. A bag of new dirt, some flowering plants that could survive on rainwater alone; it was not heavy lifting. When finished, the grave site bore all the markings of a family that cared, loved and respected the deceased.

I described earlier that in between the two Camps was the circular flower bed always well maintained by John. In this garden stood two large, black-metal, pedestal-style flower urns about four-feet tall. As a child I thought they were awesome. I had never seen anything like them before. I would watch John meticulously care for each plant in the urn and note his look of satisfaction when finished.

Generally I was not in Kingston for Memorial Day. But in early June, when I sometimes was there, I got to go with Gordon to service a cemetery urn. It was a peaceful thing to do. We enjoyed a relaxed and pleasant conversation. It was always a positive experience for us both. .

One day I was explaining to my wife, Merita, about the cemetery urns in Kingston, the ones at Camp, and about how much I loved them. I told her how the urns brought to mind many wonderful thoughts and feelings. To my great surprise and delight on my next birthday, a few months later, Merita presented me with two old fashioned black pedestal urns exactly like the ones that were in the garden at Camp. What a wonderful gift. Now every spring I plant the urns with flowers and keep them in a spot of honor in my yard for all to see. Every time I walk by my urns, with their beautiful flowers, I feel as if I am remembering and honoring my Kingston family and what I learned from them.

Whenever I visit Kingston, infrequently now, to see the changes in the city and the Ashokan Reservoir, I make my way to St. Mary's Cemetery where my great grandfather, Giuseppe Garbarino, was the first to be interred in 1913. All the Garbarino and Edelmuth family members are buried there. I would like to hire someone to neaten all the gravesites but no one performs this service anymore. Many cemeteries actually regulate against such maintenance and decorations. I feel a sense of loss but I can do nothing about it. Now my garden urns serve as their enduring and living memorial for me.

J. Garbarino International

Another element of store business John and Gordon carried into retirement after 1960 was the sale of Christmas trees.

I knew that John and Gordon, and their father before them, had a huge Christmas tree business at 784 Broadway. I have found years of newspaper references about Christmas tree donations by the J. Garbarino store to various local charities, mentioning Joseph Garbarino and later Assunta and John Garbarino. The same could be said for the Gotelli store on Front Street.

When the store was open, Christmas tree sales were profitable and a great economic addition when farm-fresh fruits and vegetables were no longer available. After the store closed in 1960, they maintained their custom of selling Christmas trees in Kingston. A small newspaper advertisement in the Kingston Daily Freeman informed their customers where their Christmas tree lot would be located that year. Selling Christmas trees served more now as a social reunion of sorts for John and Gordon with their old store customers. It was not about money. This was an important time of the year for them. They could be briefly connected to people they had known for many years.

As a child, I was sometimes in Kingston before Christmas when the Christmas trees were being sold at the store. I remember I was given a red plaid wool shirt to wear, just like Gordon wore. It was a shirt hunters wore. I felt like a real hunter. It was cold. I also was given a pair of leather gloves with woolen inserts to protect my hands from the cold and the trees. What kid wouldn't have a great time doing this? I think of these pleasant times every time I buy a Christmas tree.

The year is 1964. It is summer. I had just purchased my first new car. It was the new automotive sensation called a Ford Mustang. It was one of the first to hit the road and was an instant success with the motoring public. It was really a Ford Falcon, which had been around for years and was well tested, but now it had a new and great looking body placed over its older workings. I was hot stuff and ready for a road trip. Where to go? Well, of course, I had to share my excitement with the folks in Kingston. Thereafter, I would visit New England, never having been there before.

I visited John and Gordon at Camp along with Aunt Mamie and Uncle Bill at 8 Clinton Avenue. I had my new car and one year of college left. Life was great. One day John took me aside and explained he had been buying a truckload of Christmas trees for years from a man named Aimee Valle of Stornoway, Canada. It was supposedly not too far over the border into Canada. Since I was "going that way," John wanted to know if I would visit with Valle, check out the area for drought, and determine the condition of this season's trees. John had heard there was a drought in Canada this past summer and he did not want to purchase an entire trailer of trees that were dried out. He would have to find a new source within a short period of time if Valle's farm was part of the drought area.

I asked John if he had spoken with Valle about this drought. John looked at me like I had two heads, as if I expected Valle would say, "Yes, my trees are dried out; you need to buy elsewhere." I could tell this was important to John. I looked at my map since he was unable to give me any directions other than a man's name and the name of the town.

When I discovered Stornoway on the map, I found it was a small village, very much in the Canadian countryside. If I went to Vermont as I planned, it was only a day or two out of my way. I told John I would go to Stornoway for him and get an answer to his question. He was immediately relieved.

The paved Canadian road on which I had been driving for a couple of hours ended just as I entered the village of Stornoway. I saw a general store. I parked to go inside and inquire within for directions to Valle's farm. I could tell no one in town had seen a Ford Mustang before. They all gathered outside around my car to ask questions about it. The car caused a minor commotion and generated some curiosity about why such a car, with Maryland license plates, and the driver would come to their village of Stornoway. With everyone gathered around, I took the opportunity to gently inquire about the summer's drought. I had seen no evidence of drought along the road driving to Stornoway so I might as well see what the folks had to say. As a group they said they had no drought in their area. They had plenty of rain the entire summer.

Still needing directions, I brought up Valle's farm and the fact that my uncle bought trees from him every year. I was told, very sincerely in my opinion, Valle was a well-respected and well-liked member of the community. His trees were doing very well and he would shortly hire people from town to help cut, bind and ship them. The directions to Valle's farm were somewhat problematic. It seems I was at the end of the paved road and Valle's farm was another ten miles down a dirt road starting from the rear of the general store. Someone astutely read the chagrined look on my face as I looked at the dirt road and back to my new Ford Mustang. Would you like to speak with Aimee by phone? We can call him for you. Absent any evidence of drought, I thought this was a good idea.

The gathering moved into the general store. I studied high school French and Latin but now realized now how little I had learned. Valle's English was as good as my French but we managed to communicate. Yes, John Garbarino of Kingston was a valued customer. Valle's trees would be excellent this year. John would be very happy with the trees Aimee would ship to him in a matter of weeks. Heads in the general store bobbed up and down in agreement. This was a community where all considered themselves participants in this international business meeting. I told Aimee I was happy for his good fortune, his wonderful community here, and that John would be glad to know how well the trees were doing this year. Hopefully they had many years of business ahead. We celebrated this successful international business conversation with tea and cookies among those gathered at the general store.

Stornoway was a great adventure. It taught me something about community, the value of a general store, and what nice people exist in the world. I telephoned my Stornoway report to John immediately. Later John told me the trees he purchased that year from Valle were the best ever. Aimee was good to his word. I had no doubt but that would be the case. I was also glad that this time I was able to do something for John. No matter what trees were sent him, John did not have to worry about a financial problem. It was just part of his nature to pay attention to all the small details of his business life. He would not slack off now, not even in "retirement."

John's Retirement Companion and Another Deer Story

Retirement brought loneliness to John. He decided he would like a dog at Camp to keep him company. It was a drastic change for John to go from an active store with many different people coming in every day to Camp life, where there was little daily society for John. Gordon could hang out playing cards with the guys at the local volunteer fire house, but that was not John's style. The reason for this particular visit by me was to spend some time with John and his newly acquired friend and companion, a rabbit hound dog. I also wanted to be with John while he was adjusting to this retirement life without Gram. I had taken a bus from Baltimore to New York City, and from there another bus to Kingston. John picked me up at the bus station

Upon entering the car I was immediately introduced to "Ringy," the rabbit hound that has been so named by John in honor of the three Ring brothers – Dan, Mike and me. I am honored. Ringy accompanies John everywhere and makes a perfect companion. I immediately noted that retirement had not improved John's driving habits!

During the evening John lays on the couch watching a very grainy black and white TV. Gordon had erected a steel tower next to the new Camp to place an antenna high enough to enable John's TV watching. It never worked well.

Ringy jumps up on the couch and lies on top of John. They make a comfortable pair. By this time, most of John's conversation with me was about Kingston's past. He did not seem to have high hopes for its future. All viable business seemed to be moving outside the city, which was left to fend for itself with what was left.

I gave John much credit because he never complained. He lost the two things to which he had devoted his life, Gram and the store, at about the same time. Camp itself seemed to have lost its energy. I had to realize that just being present with John and Gordon, even for a short period, was what I could give and what they needed.

I was eighteen at the time of this visit, which generated yet another "deer story." However, it concerns only a paper deer and how I won first prize at the local volunteer fire department turkey shoot.

To raise money, the local volunteer fire department put on an outing that included various forms of target shooting contests. Gordon hung out with this volunteer fire crowd so he was called upon to help them work this turkey shoot (which by the way has nothing whatsoever to do with shooting a turkey; it is only the prize).

The visit was concluding and I left the Camp with John, who would drive me to the bus station. We stopped by the turkey shoot so I could say goodbye to Gordon. He was working the last event of the turkey shoot, which is the most difficult shooting contest of the day. It was called the "running deer." It consisted of a paper picture of a deer, mounted on a large piece of cardboard, which is attached to a pulley where the "deer" can be quickly drawn across the shooters view. The object was for the shooter to fire one shot for each ticket purchased to win the grand prize, which of course was the turkey.

I wanted to support Gordon's cause so I bought one ticket. My turn came and I fired a .22 caliber rifle with open sights. I observed there was great interest in this event by the locals as they kept track of each shot fired. It is clear that the winner of this event was considered to be something of a local shooting champion until next year's event.

After I shoot, an inquiry is yelled out from behind me, "Whad he do?"

Now the paper deer has a circle close to where a real heart would be located. Within that circle there are lines so it can be accurately determined whose shot was the closest to the center of the heart. The reply to the question is that my shot was dead through the middle of the heart and was by far the leading shot of the event.

I saw Gordon snicker a little as the "local" competition was being bested by his grandnephew from Baltimore (a city person no less). I was asked if I would like to shoot again. "Why?" I said, "The deer is dead. I wouldn't waste a second shot." Gordon snickered again. I outshot them all and walked away without comment. Was it a lucky shot or was it real talent? They could think what they wanted.

I asked Gordon to accept my prize turkey for me as I had to catch my bus. He smiled. We both got it.

The Complexities of Retirement

As a child, a teen, and sometimes even as an adult, saying goodbye to those I loved in Kingston at the end of a visit was a dreaded event for me. Only five more days; only three days left; tomorrow. The countdown could not be avoided. How many of us even now count the number of days left in our vacation? It is a painful process that I recall vividly to this day. Perhaps the issue then was more of a concern about a loss of activity and a freedom for me as a child that I did not have at home.

Along the way, as I grew older, I still felt the pangs of parting but it was less about me and more about leaving people with whom I would like to stay and help. I could make their lives easier with my physical strength, stamina, and will to see them have no worries about who would be there for them. But by now I had incurred obligations of my own through school sports, needed summer jobs, girlfriends, and social activities with my friends. All this was now in competition with Kingston. When I was married, and later became an FBI agent starting a family, the desire for Kingston was still there. It is easy enough to want to do something but competing responsibilities did not always favor Kingston.

The loss of 784 Broadway in 1960 was the start of changes I greatly disliked and even feared. I knew there was never going to be a solution that would make me happy. My family in Kingston was getting older. John and Gordon were retired. Many of their habits I knew during my childhood changed, as was consistent with their normal aging process. A visit with them now meant a lot of sitting and talking about the past.

On the more humorous side, I noted John's ability to drive a car, while never good, was now even more challenged. To say the least, he was always a rotten driver. Since the only place he seemed to drive at this point was to church on Sunday morning, there was little chance of meeting other vehicles on country Route 28A at seven o'clock on a Sunday morning. John wanted to drive me to church. I could not refuse him. At least he was a slow driver.

This church in West Hurley was a mission church of St. Joseph's in Kingston and used the same name. For John, he was continuing in the country version of his same Kingston church. John told me the priest who came to this wooden chapel, to say an early Sunday Mass, called him "the Pope." It seems John bore a striking resemblance to the then-current Pope. The chapel was too small to really sit in the back and John seemed more comfortable with this Mass now than he did at St. Joseph's in Kingston years earlier. I noted the priest always had a kind word for John after Mass. John introduced me, as he always had, "this is my sister's son's boy." As he did when I was a child, he stood a little taller and spoke with confidence when making the introduction. I was very happy John was comfortable in this country chapel with a very kind priest in attendance. On later visits, I would hear the priest say, "Well, we have the Pope with us again today." John loved it and I loved seeing him with a well-deserved moment of his own happiness.

My First Cookout

Some of my learning from Uncle Bill was more pragmatic. I recall as an adult being invited to Uncle Bill's House for a "cookout." It was 1964 and I had not heard this term used before. Uncle Bill was the first person I knew to build a backyard stone patio just below the dining room window. It was small and covered by a canvas canopy, in case of rain. It was very comfortable on a warm summer's evening. Uncle Bill had a metal grill with what I learned contained charcoal burning in it. He was going to cook the fish over the grill. When the cooking was complete, Uncle Bill took the hot coals and poured them into a bucket of water to put them out. After the steam subsided, he then dumped the coals onto a screen mesh so they could dry for later reuse. These were people that lived through a Depression and wasted nothing. Charcoal could be reused. It was a lovely dinner. It was another adventure learning to cook outside by charcoal, one that I would quickly adopt.

This form of outdoor grilling was the start of the movement away from the large stone outdoor fireplaces, like the one at the old Camp, where a wood-fire heated a large metal plate on which the cooking would be done. Certainly, the large fireplace was more work and not all backyards now had room for such fireplaces. Families also were participating in more active forms of entertainment and the rapidly developing TV world.

Uncle Bill also had what we might call today a "man cave." In the basement of 8 Clinton Avenue there was an old, unused coal bin whose chute opening to the outside driveway was now converted into a small window. The former coal bin space inside was converted into a "studio" for Uncle Bill. I noted, going down the cellar stairs from the kitchen, that many of the vertical support posts were trees that had their bark stripped and were inserted as pole supports without further refinement. They were of various diameters, not fully straight, but they had done their job well for the last seventy years. The entrance to Uncle Bill's studio was through a Dutch door, which was new to me. The bottom half of the door could be closed to keep in some heat and the top opened to allow for additional light from the stairwell. Upon entering, one would note a level floor had been installed and some walls erected to make the coal bin into a comfortable space about ten feet by twelve feet.

This is where Uncle Bill worked on his projects, stored his memorabilia, did his writing, read when not in the living room, and most importantly, did his oil painting. It was not until I was a little older that I was able to note and absorb the essence of this space. Later, I realized this was the room where I could find Uncle Bill's soul. When he painted at his easel, he wore a jump-suit garment that managed to collect samples of his oil paints before they reached the canvas or his clothing. Later I realized that his jump suit was the same color and design as the one worn by Winston Churchill as he worked about his beloved country home of Chartwell located in Kent, South East England. Besides the easels and half-finished paintings lying about, I remembered two black railroad oil lanterns that hung on the two vertical "trees" on either side of the Dutch door entrance. These lanterns reminded me of a Sherlock Holmes scene set in a romantic and always foggy London evening. They are an important part of my life today when I sit outside on summer evenings.

Aunt Mamie and Uncle Bill Watch Our High School Football Game

In 1958, I was a sophomore at the Xaverian Brothers' Mount Saint Joseph High School in Baltimore. My brother Dan was a senior at the same school, and we both played varsity football. I was the center and he played guard next to me. He was an All-Maryland selection, as I also would be at the end of the year. The local sports media covering our games liked to talk about the "two Ring brothers" who were gaining a solid football reputation. My parents would send some of the news clippings to Uncle Bill and Aunt Mamie.

Uncle Bill and Aunt Mamie decided they would drive from Kingston to Maryland to view one of our games. I thought then, and continue to think today, what good sports they were to put forth this effort. We happened to be playing another high school in the Washington, D.C. area. The opposing team was another Catholic high school, named Bishop John Carroll. It was a tough game played early in the season where we had to endure the Washington heat and humidity. I sustained a cut just under the eye that looked worse than it was. My jersey had some blood on it. On defense, my brother and I were down lineman in the center where John Carroll kept running the ball trying to wear us down in a close game. According to Aunt

Mamie, every time there was a giant collision in the middle of the line, the announcer was calling out one of the Ring names. Aunt Mamie made it to the start of the second half but was so nervous for us she had to leave and sit in the car.

At the end of the game, Aunt Mamie explained she had to go back to the car after the public address announcer kept mentioning the Ring brothers, after she observed my bloodied jersey, and how, fearing for our lives, she could not bear to watch. When I got home from the hospital after getting a few stitches, I got a big hug from Aunt Mamie. Uncle Bill said he was proud of his grandnephews but thought he and Aunt Mamie never wanted to see another one of our games.

I was so impressed that they would care enough to drive from Kingston just to visit us and see a game. They may not have had their own children but they had all of us. It certainly made me happy.

The Aging Process Marches On

I was in Baltimore for a family visit in 1970 when Gordon called. John had suffered a stroke and was unconscious in the intensive care unit of the Benedictine Hospital in Kingston. Would he live? They didn't know. I left Baltimore the next day and drove to Kingston to visit John before returning to work in Massachusetts.

I arrived at the hospital late in the evening and went alone to John's room. There was not much information to be had. They did not know if he would ever wake up. They did not know if there was any stroke damage. They would know nothing more until, if and when, he awakened.

I entered the room. There were no sounds. It was as if he and I were alone, the last inhabitants on earth. He lay in the bed curled into a fetal position. Here was one of my heroes, a strong, compassionate, loving man, now lying in a coma with no certain medical hope he would ever come out of it. His physical vulnerability and weakness were now in full bloom. He was helpless. He looked so vulnerable. In fact, his present condition proved his vulnerability. I held his hand. I spoke to him hoping somehow he could hear me. I worried what if he can hear me and just can't respond. I talked to him as if he were listening. I could not recall ever having a more lonely feeling then I did at this moment.

As I drove back to Massachusetts that evening, I prayed for John and Gordon, but I didn't know what specific outcome to pray for. If John woke up, what faculties would he have? I wanted him to have everything as it was before. I could see the future. My world of a loving Kingston was being destroyed by the aging process. You just cannot pray for that to go away. It is not realistic.

Eventually John did wake up, was mentally sound, able to walk, but was fully blind. He could no longer see and never again would. John was initially placed in a nursing home in Waterbury, Connecticut, until a public nursing home bed in Kingston became available. I went to see John once he was settled in at Waterbury. He seemed comfortable, reasonably happy, and did not complain. After being able to report to John the well-being of the rest of the folks, along with his dog Ringy, there was not a lot to talk about. The people around him were very nice and attentive.

As John's medical condition continued to improve, except for the blindness, John was relocated to a nursing home in Kingston. I found it extremely challenging and most depressing to visit John at the nursing home. I went to speak with Gordon.

"I know you and John have saved your money from all your hard work over the years. I know you are frugal and saving your money to pass on to the Ring family when you die. You have never spent any money on yourselves ever. Please don't continue with this plan. Use all your money to take John out of the nursing home and hire sufficient help to enable John to live here at Camp, in comfort, with you for the rest of your lives. This is where he belongs. You both should be together, not alone. Our family can and will make its own way."

Gordon very gently began to explain to me why this could not happen. It was Gordon's wish also to have John at Camp, but it was not possible. Gordon said it might be what he and I wished for, but that did not mean it was what John wanted. Gordon said John was already "institutionalized."

The word struck me. I sensed what he meant immediately. "John knows he is in a safe, caring environment and that is more important to him than being at Camp. I have spoken with his doctors and this will not change. Gram was blind but could live at home totally confident of our ability to provide for her daily care and keep her an important member of our store life. John's physical and emotional response to the sudden blindness does not allow him to live at Camp with the same degree of security, confidence and comfort that he presently feels in the nursing home. He has more society and people to interact with than he did at Camp."

I just stared at Gordon, trying to absorb what he was saying. Gordon continued "I have also spoken with John at length and I know this is how he feels. He does not want to leave. He is content with his nursing home environment and we must accept that."

My sadness was without measure, so deep, and the moment profound. I realized something had happened that would be forever. I would never again see John lying on the couch at Camp watching television with his beloved dog Ringy lying on top of him. He and I would not stroll the Camp grounds to see how the flower gardens were doing. We would not go for an evening ride to see where the deer were grazing. We would not get an ice cream cone as we did with Gram in the past when she was blind. It was all the small things we would never do again that depressed me. I tried to be thankful that at least John was alive and still present for visiting. It worked in theory but not in practice. Like John, I never fully recovered.

I went to the nursing home in Kingston with Gordon and Larry Machione, our close family friend. I wrote John letters, but he could not write back. Sometimes an aide would write a note for John in response to my letter. John was the first to suffer a life altering medical event. He remained in the nursing home, the last remaining Garbarino, until he died in 1979.

The Death of Uncle Bill

Uncle Bill, at age seventy-nine, was the first of the Kingston family to die (1972) after Gram (1959). I remember his funeral well. I never saw so many people during calling hours. The line was endless. All of the Ring family was there, as well as distant, surviving Edelmuth relatives. All of the Kingston and Hudson Valley community came to pay their respects to Aunt Mamie and to honor the lifetime work of Uncle Bill. Without question, all would agree it was a wonderful service for a good man for whom death came too soon.

It is ironic that Uncle Bill dropped dead from a heart attack inside a Florida pharmacy while picking up his heart medication. Present with him was my first cousin and another grandnephew, Mark Ring, son of my uncle Jack. Uncle Bill and Aunt Mamie were again visiting Florida for the winter.

As was his winter custom, he drove from Kingston to Baltimore, where they stopped to visit my mother and father, and then drove on to Florida where he stayed nearby his nephew Jack Ring (my father's brother) now working at NASA and living in Florida.

Also living in this area was my brother Dan and his family. Uncle Bill and Aunt Mamie had two families to watch over them when they came to Florida in the winter.

As I got older, I had to devote more time to summer jobs and eventually worked and went to school full time and had even less flexibility. I did not always visit Kingston for the length of time I did as a child. I did correspond with John and Uncle Bill by letter.

I followed Uncle Bill's efforts with Gateway Industries, the Mother Cabrini Home in West Park, and his now advanced hobby of oil painting. No one had ever given me an oil painting before. Uncle Bill gave me several, which I still have. I initially knew nothing about oils but over the years Uncle Bill sparked my interest in his hobby of oil painting.

Someone asked me if Uncle Bill was a "good" painter. I didn't know how to answer the question, as I never thought of his paintings in terms of competence or artistic quality. After thinking the question over, I can only say I have three of his original paintings. One I proudly gave to my grandson, and the other two have always been on display. Each time I look at them, I smile and think warmly of Uncle Bill. Therefore, I conclude he was a great painter.

I have commented before about Uncle Bill's clothing. He was not a dandy by any means, but was the most well-dressed man I knew. As I started to need my own ties, tweed sport coats, wool slacks, and dress shoes, I could and did imitate his look. His look also included more than clothing. He created a presence. He was not loud and did not try to dominate a conversation. But when he did speak, he always had something interesting or worthwhile to say. A smile was never a stranger to his face.

Uncle Bill, a voracious reader, always surrounded himself with books. I was now an avid reader so I started to look at what he was reading. It was a lot, and eclectic in scope. He was reading histories to mysteries and everything in between. I noticed how thoroughly he read the evening paper. He was interested in what political and business leaders thought. He knew the world was changing quickly after World War II and he was intent on keeping up with these changes and being part of the exciting future he saw on the horizon.

Uncle Bill viewed an unknown future with a welcoming excitement. From him I learned not to fear change, but to embrace it.

Even greater than Uncle Bill's admiration for FDR was his admiration and respect for Winston Spencer Churchill. From Uncle Bill, I also developed a curiosity about this man Churchill. When I started high school, I read, over time, William R. Shirer's *The Rise and Fall of the Third Reich*. In my own naïve way, I could not understand how or why other world governments allowed this bully Hitler to continue. Where were all the good family people of Europe? How could they let this happen? From a child's perspective, reading a very adult book, I was trying to figure out where all the good people were, and why were they silent?

I wondered why among the world's posh political leaders Churchill's was often the lone voice unwilling to appease Hitler. I began to observe the pattern of world "leaders" being willing to go along with Hitler to avoid confrontation. But not Churchill! He was willing to say what he thought about Hitler's insatiable demands. Churchill made no effort to appease Hitler. Uncle Bill introduced me to Churchill, and I have found him a worthy study when it comes to public character.

I had conversations with Uncle Bill that opened new worlds to me. It was a world of adult conversations based on knowledge. It made me want to learn. As I read about Winston Churchill, I began to realize how much of Churchill I saw in Uncle Bill. When I had dinner now with Aunt Mamie and Uncle Bill, I began to appreciate the art of dinner conversation. My conversations with Uncle Bill were often on contemporary topics. What was happening now that we had to contend with Russia? Whose side was France on? Did all business leaders want to emulate the IBM model? Why were the impoverished and mentally challenged left to fend for themselves?

How I wished, years later, that I had asked Uncle Bill more about his early years growing up, about his family, and what it was like to be the oldest and have your father die when you are a young child.

How was it when his mother had to take in boarders in order to support the family and keep a roof over their heads? How did he feel when he had to start working at thirteen and had a full time job as a traveling tobacco salesman at age sixteen? What was it like to go from being a child to a working adult almost overnight? I learned what I know now about his early days as a child growing up in Brooklyn, not from him, but from research. How did he come to be the man he was? It was not until he was gone that I realized I had not asked him many of the important questions.

As to Uncle Bill's funeral, the weather was beautiful; the wake was enormous; the funeral Mass packed; the procession to Saint Mary's Cemetery was very long. My children were ages five and seven but they remember nothing of Uncle Bill or his funeral. I am sorry they never had the opportunity to know him. I tried to explain my love for Uncle Bill to my children, and what example he offered me, but the subject just did not translate well at that age.

Aunt Mamie and Gordon at 8 Clinton Avenue

With John in a nursing home, and Uncle Bill gone, Gordon left Camp and moved in with Aunt Mamie at 8 Clinton Avenue, as both desired not to live alone. I visited Aunt Mamie and Gordon from time to time at 8 Clinton Avenue, but I could never bring myself to spend any time in Uncle Bill's studio. Aunt Mamie delicately inquired if there was anything in Uncle Bill's studio that I might like to take with me. My first instinct is to dissuade anyone from thinking I want something. I told her no. What I could not articulate was that this room was presently a sad place for me. I wanted to see it, to visit it, to remember Uncle Bill, but the sadness I felt did not encourage anything else.

I now began to see for the first time that Aunt Mamie was also old. One day I observed Aunt Mamie come down the stairs from the second to the first floor, walking backwards. I said nothing. Aunt Mamie smiled when she got to the bottom. "I don't want to fall down the stairs and this way is easier."

I smiled at her in admiration of her attitude and her response to a physical challenge. She had grit. At the same time, I could feel another cruel stab from that blunt knife of old age. Every day she went about her household duties without complaint. Without Uncle Bill to wait on, her heart was just not in it.

After Aunt Mamie and Gordon lived together for four years, she died in January of 1976. I can imagine only that the gates of heaven flew open immediately upon her arrival and that Uncle Bill was there waiting to introduce her around.

I visited Gordon several times at 8 Clinton Avenue where he was now living alone. John was still in the nearby nursing home. The absence of Aunt Mamie's care and attention to her house was greatly noticeable. It was as if the house itself was now half dead. With Aunt Mamie gone, and John in a comfortable nursing home, Gordon did not care anymore.

Gordon had been ill for some time and during our last visit, a few months prior to his death, we both knew it was probably our final visit.

Gordon had positioned a semi-comfortable chair in a dining room window that looked down the driveway and onto Clinton Avenue. There he spent most of his time just watching life go by. This was now about the extent of his world. Larry Machione was a constant visitor and, thankfully, guardian over Gordon.

As Gordon and I talked, we both knew the immediate future was not hopeful for Gordon. In truth, he did not seem to care. John was being cared for and there was nothing left for this sick old man. It would have been unkind to Gordon for me to pretend this was not the case. We said our goodbyes then. I can remember my sadness as I drove alone back to Boston across the Massachusetts Turnpike. I spoke to God on Gordon's behalf. It was the only thing I could do for him. Gordon died in October of 1976, just months after Aunt Mamie.

When Gordon died, I was on a special assignment in the Boston area, which I thought would end shortly. I intended to immediately drive to Kingston for Gordon's funeral. My parents, my two brothers and their families, were already in Kingston. The case on which I was working dragged on and late the night before the funeral, I called my father to tell him I was not coming. During the early morning hours the case was resolved somewhat and my boss told me I should go directly to the funeral. It was too late. I had no energy or desire to do so.

As I later thought about it, I realized I had said my goodbyes to Gordon privately. I did not want to be in Kingston now. I felt at the time there was now only death, decay and destruction in my favorite environment. My good memories were important and I wanted to keep them intact for a while. I wanted these people not to leave this world. I was unable and more probably unwilling to share my grief with anyone. I needed time to rid myself of the anger that came from knowing my Camelot time in Kingston was forever over.

After Gordon's funeral, my family cleared out all the personal effects at 8 Clinton Avenue to prepare the house for sale. My mother called me to ask what I wanted out of the house. My answer was nothing. I could and would not name objects as being replacements for Uncle Bill, Aunt Mamie, and now Gordon. I didn't realize at the time why I was intentionally choosing a path of rejection and avoidance. It would be a while before positive thoughts about Kingston returned.

Camp Life – A New Beginning

Gordon and the entire family had loyal and devoted friends in Larry Machione and his wife Joan, a nurse. They were just wonderful over the years in helping John, Gordon and Aunt Mamie as they progressed through their aging process and medical challenges. What a blessing it was for me to know there was someone on site constantly looking after this clan. It was Larry who kept me apprised of their medical conditions and was the person I too would come to count on.

After Gordon's funeral, my mother informed me that my father and his brother Jack inherited the old and new Camps as one property. They intended to keep both Camps for the two families to continue the tradition of "Camp." I thought this was great. Kingston will have a future. I live only three-and-a-half hours away. My children are nine and eleven years old. They will get to experience some of what I know as Camp.

A short while later my mother informs me my father and uncle Jack have decided instead to sell the Camp property. In fact, she tells me the property is actually in the process of being sold. I am quite upset and pointed out that if they we going to sell the Camp, they should have told me first and I would have bought the property. My father has not spoken directly to me on this subject. Why not? I am next told that my father and Jack are selling the Camp property to Larry and Joan Machione.

I am now both sad and happy. I am greatly saddened that my time at Camp is gone forever. I will never be able to explain Camp to my children, who are still too young now to understand. My grandchildren, when they come along, won't understand Kingston and its influence on me. An important part of my life, which I would like them all to know, is gone.

However, I am very happy for Larry and Joan. They had five children. Larry and Joan cared for our family with kind and generous hearts. They were there when we were not. Now their family would have a wonderful home and, hopefully, develop their own Camp traditions.

I learned it was my Uncle Jack's idea to sell the Camp property to Larry and Joan. He wrote a letter to my father, which I found years later, stating he thought they deserved that much for their years of effort to the Garbarino family. I agreed with Jack's sentiment wholeheartedly. Jack was living in Florida and would never have the time and ability to use the Camp the way our family would, living so much closer. An agreement was reached between Larry, my father and Jack. Larry and Joan moved into the new Camp. They continued to rent the old Camp to a long-term tenant who had rented from John and Gordon for years.

I often told Larry how happy I was for him and Joan and how much I agreed with what was done. Larry had been part of the Camp scene for years. He knew its spirit and its inheritance. Now his children would share this wonderful experience.

Camp was not going to die because the Garbarino and Edelmuth clans had come to an end. Camp was going to continue to give life, meaning and happiness to another family, other generations. Its spirit was not dead, it was just moving on. This knowledge made me very happy.

The Last Lion

John Garbarino passed away in his Kingston nursing home in May of 1979. Again, it was Larry Machione who kept the family watch and made the funeral arrangements. My father was ill and could not travel to John's funeral. I brought my twelve-year-old son Brian with me to John's funeral. Brian had visited Camp when younger but had little memory of Kingston. We stayed with Larry and Joan at the new Camp. It was a bittersweet reunion. I continued to be happy to see Camp in the hands of the Machione family.

I failed to realize this was Brian's first funeral and would be the first time he viewed a deceased person. Seeing John in his casket distressed him. It gave us a chance as father and son to talk about life and death.

The funeral Mass was held at St. Joseph's Church in Kingston, where John and I used to attend Sunday Mass. My grandparents were married there as were Aunt Mamie and Uncle Bill. Present for John's funeral Mass were Brian, Larry and myself. I kept looking around for all the many others whom I thought would read the obituary and would surely want to honor John and attend his funeral Mass? It was clear after a while that the three of us would be the only attendees at this Mass. I leaned over and asked Larry, "Where is everyone? I can't believe after the good John did throughout his life, no one is here." I was getting upset.

Larry looked at me as if I had just dropped in from Mars. "Jim, all his people, all those who would have known John, are dead. There is no one left. He is the last of his era. John was 89 and he outlived them all. There is no one else alive left to come."

Over the years Larry and I remained friends. When my daughter Diane was being sworn into the New York Bar in Albany, we stopped to pay Larry and Joan a visit at Camp. We spent an afternoon sitting out on the new porch Larry put on the front of the new Camp and catching up on life around the Ashokan Reservoir.

Later, Merita and I attended their son's wedding in Kingston. It was like being part of another wonderful family. I was able to connect his son in coming to law school in Boston. When his son graduated, Merita and I got to show Larry, Joan and their family our Italian North End of Boston. I followed Larry's progress as he remodeled the new Camp over the years to suit his family's living needs and to correct some original construction problems. I got to follow his children and their friends develop their own life and customs at Camp. I do know Camp remained a wonderful and shared environment for many.

After Larry passed away, I was told Joan intended to sell the Camp and move back to Kingston to live among her friends. Camp could be too solitary for an individual alone.

I have driven by the Camp over the years just to see what it is like. I have no idea who owns the buildings now. The actual physical connection is severed. I am thankful for all the memories that are alive and well with me.

Postscript

We may no longer sit around the traditional campfire sharing the stories and events that often became building blocks in our character formation. Today we chat on cell phones, Skype, text, Facebook, but most importantly, we continue telling our stories. They are no less valuable because we now use different means to tell them. The important thing is we continue to tell our stories. In turn, others tell us about those who were influential in their lives. "That reminds me of Uncle Ibrim who grew up in South Africa and saw ….," and we are off to learn about someone who was important to them and why. We form better human bonds through this sharing. We are not in this life alone. Our sharing expands the value of those who influenced us as news of them can now reach a wider community. Today we have the opportunity to sit around an electronic campfire, tell our stories, listen to those of others, broaden our horizons, and pay honor.

About the Author

James Ring is the author of the novel *Necessary Assets*. Ring is a retired FBI Supervisory Special Agent who investigated the American La Cosa Nostra and the Sicilian Mafia in New England. He received the Department of Justice's highest award as the architect of the first and only electronic interception of the La Cosa Nostra/Mafia induction ceremony of new members, including the Omerta oath.

Ring has testified in federal court as an expert witness on La Cosa Nostra and has served as a media commentator on organized crime. He participated in a series by National Public Radio analyzing the Department of Justice Informant Guidelines. Ring served on the Department of Defense advisory board mandated by Congress to review their civilian and military investigative capabilities. This review included the growing military preference of favoring electronic intelligence over human intelligence.

After retiring from the FBI, Ring founded a business information and investigative service within a prestigious Boston law firm. Ring now devotes his full time to writing.

Ring resides in Boston and South Dartmouth, Massachusetts, with his wife Merita A. Hopkins.

Contact Jim Ring via his website at www.jamesring.com or by email at james@jamesring.com.

About the Cover

Giuseppe "Joseph" Garbarino opened his business at 784 Broadway in 1894, and the cover photo was taken around 1900. The store in this photograph looks exactly as it did the last time I saw it in 1959.

Joseph Garbarino is standing in front of the store. The boy standing behind him is one of the young men who hung around the store, so to speak, and assisted my uncles from time to time. They were not employees. Years later I realized these boys were disadvantaged in one way or another. I remember they always left with a bag of groceries to take home to their family along with a few dollars for their day's effort.

Gram is on the far left of the photo with her daughter Lizzy alongside.